Scotland's Greatest Storyteller

The Life of Sir Walter Scott

by
Alasdair Hutton

I would like to dedicate this book
to my brother and sister Guthrie
Hutton and Fiona Anderson.
Guthrie has created a quite
remarkable number of books
about towns and industries all
over Scotland and Fiona has
kept alive the beautiful art of
craft bookbinding for many
discerning collectors. I am
proud of them both.
A.H

INTRODUCTION

Sir Walter Scott was one of the most remarkable men Scotland has produced in its long, colourful history. Born in Edinburgh in 1771, he became one of the great storytellers; commemorated by The Scott Monument in the city's Princes Street Gardens, one of the world's largest monuments to a writer.

Among his ancestors were Borders reivers, from the turbulent times when men from rival families living in the English and Scottish borderlands would ride out at night in groups to steal livestock and anything else they could lay their hands on.

Growing up listening to tales of these ancestors meant Walter Scott had a passion for history, coupled with a vivid imagination, telling glorious stories with a huge cast of memorable characters. His writing popularised many images and phrases that we still use today.

In this sweep across an astonishingly full and busy life you will glimpse what made Sir Walter Scott stand head and shoulders above his contemporaries, and why he was read and admired across the world. I hope it will tempt you to explore his stories and poems for yourself.

Sir Walter's beloved home at Abbotsford has been restored and is open to the public. I would urge you to visit it. The Edinburgh Sir Walter Scott Club, established in 1894, exists to let people know more about the great man, and all the nooks and crannies of his extraordinary life, attracting some of the best-known names in literature and society to explain why they love Scotland's greatest storyteller.

2021 is the 250th anniversary of Scott's birth, and this book was created to celebrate his life and works; hopefully encouraging you to appreciate the great man and everything he did for Scotland.

2022 is Scotland's Year of Stories, a year in which stories inspired by, created, or written in Scotland will be showcased and celebrated. What better time to celebrate the life of Sir Walter Scott?

Alasdair Hutton
Kelso, 2021

Chapter One

In which Walter is born,
and promptly nearly
dies (several times).

On the 15th of August 1771, the baby who was to become Scotland's greatest storyteller was born in Edinburgh. He was christened Walter Scott.

Although he was born in Scotland's capital city, his ancestors came from the Scottish Borders. Scott is a famous name in those parts and the head of the Scotts, His Grace the Duke of Buccleuch continues to live there. The baby's father was called Walter, like a great many of his forebears, so it was quite natural that the child would carry the same name on into the next generation.

Walter's father was a lawyer of a type known in Scotland as a Writer to the Signet, and a handsome man with a kind and generous manner. He was a just, honourable, and conscientious man, and although he was the first of his family to move to the city, he always retained a warm affection for the Borderland.

Walter's mother Anne was the daughter of a distinguished Professor of Medicine at Edinburgh University and was well educated in all the accomplishments required of a young lady of the time, including reading, writing, needlework, and the keeping of household accounts. She had a poise and grace which she retained to the end of her long life.

The young Walter Scott nearly died immediately after his birth. His first nurse was suffering from a disease called consumption, now known as tuberculosis. She probably didn't know she was dangerously ill and wouldn't want to risk losing her job in such a happy household by telling

5

anyone. Before her condition was discovered the whole household was exposed to the disease, but luckily baby Walter survived and showed every sign of being strong, healthy and agile. That was until he was about eighteen months old when he caught a fever.

Four days later the toddler had lost the use of his right leg.

Walter's parents asked for help from several prominent doctors in the city but none of them could work out what was wrong with the child as there was no dislocation or sprain. Growing increasingly anxious, they grasped at every prospect of a cure. The experts suggested treatments that sound barbaric to us. One of them even believed that blistering of the skin, particularly the legs, was an effective cure for a variety of ailments. The poor child had to endure that and many other supposed remedies, such as regularly being bled of up to two cups of blood and having to swallow various laxatives in an attempt to rid him of the illness. But it didn't matter what the doctors tried, there was no improvement. It was a mystery!

In fact, we now know that young Walter had caught the polio virus, which was quite common at the time, and for which there was no cure.

Baffled by his grandson's illness, Dr Rutherford, Walter's maternal grandfather, suggested that the child should go to the country, for exercise and fresh air. Walter was sent to stay with his other grandfather, Robert Scott, at Sandy Knowe, a farmhouse nestling in the shadow of Smailholm Tower near St Boswells in the Scottish Borders.

There's no doubt that the countryside helped Walter to recover, but the little boy was not out of the woods yet. One of the maids who had been ordered to travel with him to Sandy Knowe desperately wanted to return to her sweetheart in Edinburgh. Broken-hearted – and presumably furious - when Walter's mother refused her permission to leave, the maid took the infant up to the crags around Smailholm Tower intending to murder him!

Fortunately, she did not go through with her plan, returning Walter safely to the house where she confessed to the old housekeeper. Unsurprisingly, she was dismissed.

At Sandy Knowe, Walter continued to be subjected to all sorts of odd attempts at a cure, one of which was to wrap the child in a warm sheep skin just after the animal had been killed. Walter's grandfather also tried lots of little tricks to encourage him to crawl, sure that the exercise would mend the weakened leg, encouraging their many visitors to help.

One of Walter's elderly relatives, Sir George MacDougal of Makerstoun, who had been a Colonel in the Scots Greys, came one day, dressed in his old military uniform. What must little Walter have thought as this elderly gentleman - wearing an embroidered scarlet waistcoat, a light-coloured coat, and a small, cocked hat, with his milk-white hair tied in a military-style ponytail - dragged his pocket watch across the floor, insisting that Walter follow it? Perhaps it's not surprising, given his early life experiences, that young Walter grew up to devise action-packed plots with large casts of full-blooded heroes and heroines.

During those years at Sandy Knowe, the little boy was often carried about among the crags on the backs of the young ewe-milkers, but his greatest pleasure was to sit on the shoulders of Sandy Ormiston, the Cow-Baillie, who was responsible for the farm's livestock. Sandy would find somewhere safe for the toddler to sit from where he could watch while Sandy supervised the flock. The "sweet-tempered bairn" soon learned to distinguish every sheep and lamb by its head mark. But even with Sandy looking after him, Walter was far from safe.

The arrangement was that the Cow-Baillie would blow a particular note on his whistle to signal to the maidservants that the child was ready to be collected. But the system didn't always work. On one occasion, the little boy was left out on the hills during a thunderstorm while everyone else ran for shelter. Remarkably, when his appalled aunt dashed out to find him the little boy was none the worse, clapping his hands at the lightning and crying "Bonny, bonny!" at every flash.

Walter was a lively, engaging child and his natural impatience and determination soon got the better of his physical limitations. Little by little he taught himself to stand up, then walk, and at last run. Even though his affected leg was shorter than the other one, his general health must have benefitted from all that open air, leading Walter to grow up a healthy, high-spirited, and sturdy child.

His parents naturally remained concerned for their son. It was the Romans who discovered that the water from the hot springs - in what is now the English city of Bath - had unusual health-giving properties. When Walter was three years old his father was advised that this water might help cure his lameness, so the child set off with his aunt, Miss Janet Scott. Janet and Walter sailed first to London in a ship called the Duchess of Buccleuch before travelling on to Bath. The young boy must have had an observant eye and a good memory, for a quarter of a century later he could still recall the details of Westminster Abbey and the Tower of London.

They lived at Bath for about a year without seeing any improvement to his withered leg, despite frequent visits to the baths. Walter rather enjoyed himself however - the baths were busy places, full of people who were taken with this precocious Scottish child.

One of them was the Reverend John Home, originally from Ancrum in the Borders, who was in Bath with his poorly wife. Mr Home had fought against the Jacobites in the 1745 uprising and the couple took the Scotts under their wing. Mrs Home liked to take the air in her carriage on the Bathampton Down, and young Walter loved to accompany her.

Walter's uncle, Captain Robert Scott, was another visitor. Walter enjoyed the elegance of the buildings and the serenity of the countryside around the city, but he preferred the splendours of a toyshop near the Orange Grove to which Uncle Robert introduced him. The boy had never seen anything like it in the Borders.

He was taken to the theatre to see William Shakespeare's play, As You Like It. It is likely that not all the theatregoers appreciated the presence of a small child. Walter later recalled making quite a lot of noise during the performance and shouting "A'n't they brothers?" during the quarrel between Orlando and his brother in the opening scene.

After a year in Bath, Walter and his aunt returned first to Edinburgh, and then to Sandy Knowe. Despite everything his leg was no better, but his parents were still determined not to give up! So, when he was seven, and someone suggested that sea bathing might provide a cure, off he went with his aunt to Prestonpans on the East Lothian coast. For several weeks he was encouraged to plunge regularly into the chilly waters of the Firth of Forth.

Despite all these efforts on their son's behalf, Walter's limp was permanent, and he would need a stick to help him walk for the rest of his life.

Leaving Prestonpans behind, Walter happily returned to Sandy Knowe. He was a sociable boy and enjoyed exploring the local area whenever he could, chatting to the many local characters who were only too pleased to be waylaid by him, happy to share their stories of heroes and heroines, villains and courageous nightriders.

The Battle of Culloden and Bonnie Prince Charlie's escape through the heather had taken place only 25 years before Walter was born. Feelings on both sides continued to run deep. One or two of his distant relations had been killed in the battle, and perhaps unsurprisingly he developed a hatred of the Duke of Cumberland who had led the King's Army against Bonnie Prince Charlie and his Jacobite soldiers. Walter's great-grandfather was always known as Beardie because of his large beard which he never trimmed to show his sorrow for the banished dynasty of Stuart kings to which Bonnie Prince Charlie belonged.

Evidence of these early influences – the old songs and ballads of the Borders, and history fresh in the hearts and minds of those who had lived it – can be seen throughout Scott's writing. He later wrote that the "green hill and the clear blue heaven" of the Scottish Borders had given him his poetic impulse. The Edinburgh of his birth was then a dirty and unhealthy place and he always believed that if he had grown up there, he would have been condemned to hopeless and helpless illness. As it was, he grew tall and strong and, connected with the history and folklore of his ancestors, destined to become a great man in the world.

CHAPTER TWO

In which Walter learns
about the world,
and discovers a love
of literature.

Walter's lively imagination had been fired by the tales he heard and the characters he met at Sandy Knowe. But to progress in the world his parents knew that he would need more than a head full of old stories, however entertaining they were.

His early education had been well-meaning but a little hit or miss. In Bath, he had learned the rudiments of reading at a day-school, kept by an old lady known in those days as a Dame, near to where he was living with his aunt – who occasionally added extra lessons.

Walter was a good listener and he loved it when his grandmother settled down to tell him the adventures of larger-than-life characters like Watt of Harden, Wight Willie of Aikwood, Jamie Telfer of the fair Dodhead, and her other Border heroes. These tales were passed down through generations, and Walter lapped up her stories and many more from the people he met when he was staying in the area, who were only too pleased to share them.

An uncle by marriage, Mr. Curle, the farmer at nearby Yetbyre, had been present at the execution of some of the defeated Jacobites captured on their retreat north. The tragic tales of those sad men made a lasting impression on the young Walter.

In Prestonpans Walter met a military veteran called Dalgetty, who had pitched his tent in the little village after returning home from the German wars. The boy loved the old man's tales of battles won and lost. He was fascinated by current affairs too and sometimes he and "Captain"

Dalgetty discussed the American wars of Independence, which were raging at the time. Walter had studied a map of North America and was struck by the rugged appearance of the country. He disagreed with the old soldier about how the war would end; and turned out to be right when, in 1783, the American colonists overthrew their British rulers and formed the fledgling United States of America.

Back in Edinburgh, Walter made a strong impression on those he met. One particular visitor to his parents' house, the lively author Alison Cockburn, described him as "the most extraordinary genius of a boy I ever saw". They had chatted about the poet John Milton and other books Walter was reading and Mrs Cockburn declared herself astonished that he was still only five, describing him as "an uncommon exotic". The feeling was mutual. Scott said he liked Mrs Cockburn because she was a "virtuoso like himself".

But Walter continued to spend much of his life at Sandy Knowe. When he was given his first pony, a tiny Shetland mare called Marion, he was able to explore more of the wider Borderland. He rode through the woods of the nearby Mertoun estate and even as far as the River Tweed, though it was too far from Sandy Knowe for him to go regularly. His love for the surrounding area increased with every outing.

There would always be two or three old books on the window seat at Sandy Knowe seeing Walter through winter days when riding out was not practical.

Automathes, the tale of a young nobleman, accidentally left alone as an infant on a desolate island until he was nineteen, and Allan Ramsay's *Tea-Table Miscellany*, a collection of old Scots and English songs and ballads, were among his favourites, although he also came to enjoy the historian Titus Flavius Josephus's *Wars of the Jews* which was to fire his imagination, probably inspiring his *Tales of the Crusaders* many years later.

With admirable patience Walter's devoted Aunt Janet would read these works to him, until he could repeat long passages by heart. His memory was extraordinary. Early on he mastered *The Ballad of Hardyknute*, a lengthy poem from the *Tea-Table Miscellany*. However not everybody appreciated the boy's contributions. Dr Duncan, the local clergyman, resented having his sober conversation interrupted by a boy shouting out lengthy extracts and once exclaimed in exasperation: "One may as well speak in the mouth of a cannon as where that child is."

When Walter was seven, he returned to live in his parents' house in George Square in Edinburgh, visiting Sandy Knowe only during the holidays. After the freedom of life in the Borders, he struggled to adapt to city life in a large family. His three brothers and sister considered him "a single, indulged brat" who was used to having his own way. It took some time, but gradually Walter learned to fit in, and he was especially glad of the help of his understanding mother who enjoyed sharing poetry and stories with him. Although she found it hard to distract Walter from the verses which described battles, which he loved, she insisted that her son pause at the gentler passages, and he learned to divide his attention between them. He continued to learn by heart the passages he liked best and used to recite them aloud, both to himself and to others, although now that he was at home in Edinburgh, he preferred to do it alone because his siblings made fun of his efforts.

His mother dreaded her youngest son going to school so she deferred the day as long as possible. But she couldn't put it off forever. They were all too aware that Walter had never learned to read properly or acquire correct pronunciation, so his parents sent him to a private school in Bristo Port in Edinburgh run by a Mr Leechman. When that was not a success his parents hired a young tutor, Mr James French who taught him a basic knowledge of Latin. This meant that he could join Mr Luke Fraser's class at the renowned High School of Edinburgh.

Walter's formal schooling began at the age of eight, in October 1779. He was younger than most of his classmates and struggled to make much progress, but three years later, in the class of the headmaster, Dr Adam, he became fascinated by Latin literature and suddenly found his academic feet. His verse translations from the Roman poets met with approval from his teachers and soon he began to write poetry of his own.

During these years he had another private tutor, James Mitchell, who later became a minister of the church at Montrose. He enjoyed engaging Walter in discussions about religion and church history and the two had lengthy, good-natured arguments.

Walter's education was not restricted to his tutor or the High School classroom. His informal education took place in the playground and on the Edinburgh streets where he was known as a bit of a fighter. These skirmishes were very common at the time, involving gangs who lived in one square or district fighting against those of a neighbouring one. They could last for a whole evening, but there was no real malice or ill-will between the youngsters. It was largely only rough play using stones, sticks and fists and in the winter, snowballs.

At school Walter was always reading and he soon became popular with his classmates as a spinner of stories. He particularly enjoyed Shakespeare, reading as much as he could lay his hands on, and any other plays, novels and poetry that came his way, and his extraordinary memory meant that he was able to quote from an impressive range of poetry and prose. He collected old ballads from his mother and his mother's friends and even began to lay the foundations of his library, buying himself cheap little pamphlets known as "chap-books" which were popular at the time.

Walter left the High School in the spring of 1783. His health still concerned his parents, so his father was easily persuaded to let him spend half a year at Kelso with his aunt, Janet. She had moved to the border town from Sandy Knowe. Her little house stood in a large garden, decorated with the complicated designs of mazes and bowers which were popular at the time. At the foot of the garden rolled the waters of the great River Tweed. Walter was in his element, and it was here that he came to know and love the river which was to figure so prominently in his later life.

He attended Kelso Grammar School, where his Latin continued to improve. But perhaps most importantly, he became firm friends with fellow-pupil James Ballantyne, the son of a local tradesman. We will see later how important that friendship was to become for both of them. In the meantime, Walter spent four hours a day at the Grammar School and the rest of his time was spent reading as much history or poetry or tales of voyages and travels as he could lay his hands on, alongside fairy tales, Eastern stories, and romances.

Walter memorised the passages which particularly appealed to him - a favourite poem, a playground rhyme, or, above all, the ballad of a Border-raid – soaking up a rich and varied vocabulary of what was striking and picturesque. He described himself at the time as being "like an ignorant gamester, who kept a good hand until he knew how to play it." He recalled how, on one evening, his delight at what he was reading under a great Oriental Plane tree in his aunt's garden so completely replaced his appetite that he forgot his dinner. When he was eventually found he was still deep in his intellectual banquet. It is clear to see that the seeds of his later writing career were being sown and nurtured with everything he read and heard.

Chapter Three

In which Walter enters
Edinburgh society
and meets
Robert Burns.

Walter's teenage years were spent back in Edinburgh. It was an exciting time to be in the city, as we shall see.

The union of the crowns of Scotland and England in 1603 had taken the royal Court, with its influence and its sycophants, away to London. The Parliaments of the two countries were dissolved in 1707 and the new parliament for Great Britain took the politicians and their attendant establishments south too.

But several of Scotland's institutions remained unchanged. Scottish law remained separate from English law, so the law courts with their lawyers and judges remained in Scotland. So too did the headquarters and leadership of the Church of Scotland and, most importantly, the country's four universities and its medical establishment. The lawyers and the ministers, together with the professors, philosophers, medical men, scientists and architects formed a new elite to create that astonishing flowering of intellectual brilliance which became known as the Scottish Enlightenment.

Such towering global figures as the philosopher David Hume, the economist Adam Smith, the mathematician Dugald Stewart and the father of modern geology James Hutton emerged as key influencers, their work encouraging lively debate. Supper became the byword for good conversation and conviviality and Edinburgh suppers were particularly renowned for their wide-ranging debates. Many took place in taverns and the groups often formed themselves into clubs, some with distinctive names and customs.

Scotland was gradually creating a network of institutions, including universities, libraries, periodicals, museums, and masonic lodges, which extended Scottish influence far beyond the borders, throughout continental Europe and across the Atlantic.

When the 27-year-old poet Robert Burns was being celebrated in Edinburgh Society, the 15-year-old Walter Scott was very keen to meet him, but he did not know anyone in literary circles who could introduce them. One day however, early in 1787, he was staying at the Sciennes home of Professor Adam Ferguson when the poet happened to be visiting. Burns seemed reluctant to mingle, moving around the room looking at the pictures and paintings that hung on the walls. When he came to a print of William Henry Bunbury's *Affliction*, a painting which showed a soldier lying dead in the snow with his dog sitting miserably on one side, his widow with a child in her arms on the other, the teenage Scott noticed him shedding tears. Underneath the print were six lines of verse which seemed to affect the poet. He turned and asked whose lines they were, and only Walter could remember that they were from a half-forgotten poem by John Langhorne called *The Justice of The Peace*. Not quite brave enough to talk directly to the great man, Walter whispered the information to another guest, who mentioned it to Burns. The poet was pleased and looked the teenager in the eye. Walter recalled noticing a strong expression of sense and shrewdness in Burns but most of all that his large, dark eyes indicated his poetical character and temperament and how he "literally glowed" when he spoke with feeling or interest. It was a memory he would cherish.

Walter's two elder brothers had chosen the Army and the Navy, so it was perhaps inevitable that Walter should pursue the third of the normal callings of a gentleman at the time, the law, and follow in his father's footsteps. His parents had suggested that he might become a minister of the church but although he was still in his early teens, Walter made it very clear that he had no interest in such a profession. So, at fourteen years of age, Walter signed up to be his father's apprentice for the next five years.

It wasn't a happy experience for a young man with a lively mind. He found himself sitting at a desk for many hours every day copying legal documents. He had little interest but applied himself diligently and showed a remarkable capacity for the solid, plodding work. The task of copying legal documents did have some advantages: all the apprentices were paid at the rate of threepence per folio, or sheet of paper, which was quite a decent sum in those days. He was a fast worker and these earnings enabled him to buy books and theatre tickets – motivation indeed. On one occasion he copied one hundred and twenty folio pages, probably about ten thousand words, without stopping for food or rest.

The work also had a long-term benefit. It gave him a good "running hand" - what we now call 'joined up writing'. Until the end of his life Walter always finished off a page with a flourish of his pen, a safeguard, his son-in-law John Gibson Lockhart believed, against a forged line being added later. Later in life, when he completed his manuscripts at Abbotsford his family would hear him say, "There goes the old shop again!", presumably meaning "old habits die hard".

The apprenticeship undoubtedly brought Walter closer to his father, but they remained very different characters. Walter's father never quite understood his son's wish to embrace a wider understanding of literature and science as part of his legal education. However, he did not try to stop him and although the ambitious young Walter disliked the drudgery and confinement of the office, he was determined to make himself useful by labouring hard and well.

Still, Walter was not quite done with illness. When he was sixteen, a burst blood-vessel in his bowels meant that he had to lie on his back for weeks in a room with the windows wide open. The potential boredom of this tough regime, to which Walter submitted without complaint, was relieved by books, specifically the extraordinary worlds of imagination created by the poet Edmund Spenser and his continuing passion for William Shakespeare. Chess was popular at the time and at first he engaged eagerly in the game with the friends, glad of their company, but he soon tired of it, deciding that "chess-playing is a sad waste of brains."

After that grim period of recuperation Walter began to outgrow the poor health of his childhood. Nothing could hold him back; he could walk thirty miles in a day and ride a horse as long as it could carry him. He grew tall and broad-shouldered, deep in the chest, and with arms like a blacksmiths. In his late 50s, Walter recalled the spirit of his youth: "There is a touch of the old spirit in me yet that bids me brave the tempest—the spirit that in spite of manifold infirmities made me a roaring boy in my youth, a desperate climber, a bold rider, a deep drinker, and a stout player at singlestick." One morning he called on a fellow law student, William Clerk of Eldin, and regaled him with a story about being set upon the night before. He was proud of having defended himself for an hour with his stick before driving the three thugs away.

At seventeen Walter began to attend lectures in Civil Law at Edinburgh University, and he was taught Scots Law by David Hume. He was in illustrious company. His classmates included William Clerk, John Irving, Adam Ferguson, George Cranstoun (later Lord Corehouse), Francis Jeffrey, George Abercromby (later Lord Abercromby), John James Edmonstone of Newton, Sir Patrick Murray of Ochtertyre, and Patrick Murray of Simprim. Some were destined to become brilliant lawyers, and several became judges.

Walter worked hard for the next three years. He was not a boastful man but later he wrote: "Let me do justice to the only years of my life in which I applied myself to learning with stern, steady, and undeviating industry."

Walter and his great friend William Clerk would examine each other upon different points of law. Every morning, except Sundays, he walked the two miles to William's house at the West End of Princes Street, and the two students worked their way through all the most important legal texts. In fact, they passed their Faculty of Advocates exams on the same day and on 11th July 1792 they each assumed the gown of an Advocate with all its duties and honours.

After the ceremony admitting them to the Faculty of Advocates before the Dean and other office-bearers, they were sworn in as officers of the court in the Outer House of the Court of Session in Edinburgh, the supreme court for civil cases in Scotland since 1532.

Now qualified, and a practising lawyer, Walter knew how to enjoy himself. Supper parties were popular and a gentleman, even one at his young age, was expected to drink his share of wine and to carry it well. When wine-fuelled quarrels broke out, as they often did, Walter was usually the chief peacemaker.

He belonged to many Edinburgh clubs. In the Literary Society his antiquarian learning won him the nickname Duns Scotus., after the 13th Century philosopher-priest. He was a member of The Club, which met in Carrubber's Close and the Teviotdale Club, where he was delighted to renew his friendship with his old Kelso schoolfriend James Ballantyne. And there was the famous Speculative Society, the membership made up largely of literary and legal talent, to which he was elected librarian and later secretary and treasurer.

Despite his growing reputation as a lawyer, Walter's love of the romantic history of his homeland was rarely far from his mind. His father had numerous Highland clients requiring professional advice, and Walter was delighted by the opportunity to travel to them to offer it. Alexander Stewart of Invernahyle in Argyll was an enthusiastic Jacobite, with vivid memories of his involvement in the insurrections both of 1715 and 1745. The young lawyer listened with eager delight to Stewart's tales of his early days, including his broadsword duel with Rob Roy, and the threat from the Galloway-born American sailor John Paul Jones to hold Edinburgh to ransom in September 1779. The old man told Walter how he had "exulted in the prospect of drawing his claymore once more before he died" but was not given the chance as Jones withdrew without a fight.

No wonder Walter looked forward to these excursions and repeated those Highland visits almost every summer for several years. They opened the romantically minded young lawyer to new places and such landscapes as the Trossachs and the vale of Perth. Both made such an impression that they later came to serve as backgrounds in his writing.

CHAPTER FOUR

In which Walter's love of the ancient ballads lead to the publication of his first books.

From the time he was an infant, living at Sandy Knowe, Scott's ears had been tuned to the rhythm and sounds of the Border tongue. What he heard developed in him a love for the old tales of his Border ancestors and the men they rode with. Scott had a fine appreciation of music, inspired by the Border ballads, the rhythm of hoof-beats and the clash of swords.

By the time Walter was born, that lawless world of cattle and sheep-raiding or reiving, as it was known along the Border, was largely over. This didn't stem his imagination however, which was fired up by the vivid images in the stories and ballads he heard and memorised. Whenever he could grab the chance of a holiday, he would set off for his beloved Borderland, to Kelso and Jeddart (Jedburgh) and to the Northumbrian side of the Cheviots, from where he wrote colourful letters to his friends and jotted down his thoughts in notebooks.

Writing was in his blood and his appetite for writing down scraps of information he came across was an instinct. He described being presented with a large old Border war-horn, which now hangs in the armoury at Abbotsford. Found in Hermitage Castle, Hawick, the original chain, hoop, and mouthpiece of steel were all complete and unbroken. The young lawyer carried his treasure home from Liddesdale to Jedburgh, slung about his neck.

Walter found it easy to chat with the shepherds, farmers and other country folk he met on his walks through the hills. Many of them would have been the descendants of the men who had answered the midnight call to go raiding over the border, returning with stolen cattle and sheep to replenish their larders when they ran low. They would have revelled in the opportunity to retell the old tales of riding by moonlight to such an eager listener. Much local history was carried from generation to generation through ballads, often exaggerated and embellished in the retelling.

What Walter understood by instinct as much as by heritage was that for centuries the Borderland had effectively been separate from the rest of Scotland and England. Borderers devised and lived by their own codes and rules as distance and rough country made it difficult and dangerous for the authorities to enforce the laws of the neighbouring lands.

Although the Borderers' laws were quite different from the law which Walter had studied, he understood the code of conduct which governed the way these reiving families had lived. Each created and followed its own signs and symbols through the countryside, the reivers moving along quiet tracks known only to themselves. The scale of the raids varied greatly - from a few dozen opportunists to sophisticated campaigns involving up to three thousand riders. Most took place during the early winter months, when the nights were longest and the livestock fat from a summer's grazing. It was dangerous work, and those caught were often sentenced to death by hanging or forced to serve as conscripts in the English and Scots armies.

Many Borderer conscripts played important roles at the battles of Flodden and Solway Moss, but they could be a mixed blessing, as they were notoriously difficult to control. Many had relatives on both sides of the border (despite laws forbidding international marriage), and they could therefore claim to be of either nationality.

At the Battle of Ancrum Moor in 1545, Borderers changed sides in mid-battle to curry favour with the likely victors, and at the Battle of Pinkie Cleugh in 1547, Scottish and English Borderers were spotted talking to each other in the midst of battle, though they put on a grand show of fighting when they realised they were being watched.

These rousing stories appealed hugely to the young Walter Scott. He was enthusiastic to hear the old ballads of the Borderland and wanted to capture the language they used which he felt was slipping away and would soon be forgotten. He must have been aware of what Robert Burns had achieved, travelling the country as an exciseman gathering old songs along the way and writing them down, often having to complete fragments using his own poetic skill. Walter took to doing this as well, and so by the time he was 25 he was already well on his way to publishing the ballads he had collected on his travels. As he wrote later, he wanted to "contribute something to the history of my native country; the peculiar features of whose manners and character are daily melting and dissolving."

Walter's old friend, James Ballantyne, was a printer in Kelso and publisher of the weekly Kelso Mail, and they found themselves travelling from Kelso on the same coach in 1797. Travel was slow then so there was ample time for talk and Walter persuaded James that he could use his printing skills to publish a book, when the presses were not busy with newsprint. James agreed and in 1799 he secretly issued two publications *An Apology for Tales of Terror*, which contained three poems translated by Scott from German, and *The Eve of St John*, an original ballad written by Scott based on an old Border legend set at Smailholm Tower. It was the first time Walter saw his writing in print and led to the rekindling of the childhood friendship of the two young men.

Chapter Five

In which Walter
explores the countryside
and falls in love.

Walter was now a qualified lawyer, and he was reasonably successful. Work was coming to him through his father's office, some in Edinburgh (where he had a reputation for defending poor prisoners without charging them) some from the Highlands, and many clients across the South of Scotland. In the Borderland, he often found himself giving a legal voice in court to poachers and sheep stealers.

On one occasion, Walter went to Gatehouse of Fleet in Galloway to investigate the case of Rev. Mr McNaught, minister of Girthon, whose trial was to take place before the General Assembly of the Church of Scotland. He had been charged with habitual drunkenness; singing lewd and profane songs; dancing with a local woman at a penny-wedding; and of promoting irregular marriages. It was the sort of case Walter enjoyed. He put up a spirited defence of the minister, even repeating his coarse language in the General Assembly Court to the horror of its members. It must have been quite a performance. His contemporaries in the gallery noisily encouraged him to go further and were promptly ejected. Walter's defence focused on there being a difference between being occasionally drunk and being an alcoholic, but however passionately he made his argument it did not save the minister.

In his first appearance as counsel in a criminal trial at Jedburgh, he helped a veteran poacher and sheep-stealer to escape through some loophole of the law. "You're a lucky scoundrel," Walter whispered to his client when the verdict was pronounced. "I'm just o' your mind," the scoundrel replied, and promised to send him a hare the next day.

At another hearing in Jedburgh even Walter's considerable legal skill failed to secure a notorious housebreaker's acquittal. The man was, however, grateful for Scott's efforts on his behalf and asked him to visit him in the condemned cell, telling him, "I am very sorry, sir, that I have no fee to offer you, so let me beg your acceptance of two bits of advice which may be useful when you come to have a house of your own. Never keep a large watchdog out of doors, we can always silence them cheaply, but tie a little, tight, yelping terrier within; and secondly, put no trust in nice, clever, gimcrack locks. The only thing that bothers us is a huge old heavy one, no matter how simple the construction, and the ruder and rustier the key, so much the better for the housekeeper." Years later Scott summed up the housebreaker's advice in rhyme:

"Yelping terrier, rusty key,
Was Walter Scott's best Jeddart fee."

When his professional life allowed it, Walter continued to explore the borderlands as enthusiastically as ever whenever he could. Over several years he made what he called "raids" into the wild countryside of Liddesdale in Roxburghshire, exploring every rivulet to its source, and every ruined peel tower from foundation to battlement. Folk there had never seen a wheeled carriage before Walter's two-wheeled gig appeared. They had only occasionally glimpsed an advocate in the area but like so many others, they took to Scott. There was something about him that made them comfortable. At one of the farmhouses he visited, Millburnholm, the farmer Willie Elliot declared him to be "just a chield like ourselves".

While Scott had been training, the French Revolution had been gathering pace on the other side of the English Channel. The full force of the overthrow of the established order and the execution of the King and members of the aristocracy shook Europe to its core. The extremist French Jacobins established a Reign of Terror characterised by constant public executions. The public became so terrified by the Jacobins' savagery that after a year they took the only action open to them and turned on the leaders, who were executed. This gave Napoleon Bonaparte his opportunity to take charge, arousing a new wave of national pride in France. Soon he turned his military gaze on the other countries around Europe, alarming their governments and people.

Britain, its regular army facing French armies in Europe and further afield, braced itself for an invasion. Prime Minister William Pitt called on every able-bodied citizen to take up arms in defence of the country.

In Edinburgh, a force of 3000 armed and disciplined volunteers was drawn from the city and surrounding counties, including a regiment of cavalry, and two corps of artillery, each capable of manning and firing twelve guns.

Scott's brother Thomas joined the Edinburgh Volunteers, but Walter's disability prevented hm from joining up so, rousing the borderland spirit of his ancestors, he inspired as many friends as he could to join the Royal Edinburgh Light Dragoons, a corps of gentleman volunteers established in 1797. Where Thomas would carry a musket, Walter would wield a sabre.

Walter was popular with his fellow soldiers, many of them gentlemen unused to 5am drills. His fine riding skills, on a powerful steed named Lenore, and his good humour kept up their spirits. Whenever they were ordered to sit at ease every eye turned to 'Earl Walter', as he was called by them, who could be relied upon to provide a morale-boosting joke. By all accounts training, though gruelling, could be good fun. Walter loved to gallop along the sands at Portobello, training his men to use their sabres by "beheading" a turnip on top of a pole, shouting "Cut them down, the villains, cut them down!" Scott even composed a War Song for his Light Dragoons. The final verse rings with patriotic fervour:

To horse! to horse! the sabres gleam;
High sounds our bugle call;
Combined by honour's sacred tie,
Our word is Laws and Liberty!
March forward, one and all!

Despite all this activity, Scott still managed to appear regularly in the Parliament House in gown and wig. And of course, he took every opportunity to read and write.

Walter was always proud of his military service and when, in Paris in 1815, after the Battle of Waterloo, Czar Alexander of Russia asked in what battles he had fought, Walter replied modestly that he had been in the volunteer cavalry and had engaged in "some slight actions such as the battle of the Cross Causeway and the affair of Moredun Mill", embellishing the truth in the traditional manner of a real Borderer, as neither area had seen any military combat.

When the Court of Session rose for the summer of 1797, Walter decided to set out on a tour of the English Lakes with his brother John and Adam Ferguson and they made their headquarters at Gilsland on Hadrian's Wall. Out riding one day the young men were struck by a young lady also on horseback. She had large brown eyes, black hair, and a charming French accent.

At a ball on the same evening Captain Scott appeared in his uniform, as did Ferguson, and was introduced properly to the beautiful young lady they had seen earlier that day. Her name was Charlotte Margaret Carpenter, and for Scott it was love at first sight.

Charlotte was the daughter of a French royalist, Jean Charpentier of Lyons. After his death, his wife, also Charlotte, had escaped with their children at the start of the Revolution and found safety with an old friend, the Marquis of Downshire. Sadly, Madame Charpentier died soon afterwards, leaving the Marquis as guardian to her children.

After their meeting at the ball, Charlotte went to stay with friends in Carlisle. Walter followed her, and romance blossomed. Walter wrote to his mother to tell her of his intention to make Charlotte his wife the couple were married in St Mary's Church in Carlisle on Christmas Eve 1797. Soon afterwards they settled down in a cottage in Lasswade, a village on the River Esk a dozen miles from Edinburgh.

1799 brought sadness, happiness, and the start of a new era.

In April, Walter's father died at the age of 69, following a long illness. October brought the happiness of the birth of the couple's first child, Sophia. Then towards the end of the year Andrew Plummer, a good friend of Walter's who happened to be the Sheriff-depute of Selkirkshire, died. At the recommendation of the Duke of Buccleuch, Walter Scott was asked to be Sheriff-depute.

So, on 16 December Walter was appointed as Sheriff-depute of Selkirkshire. In Scotland a Sheriff is a judge, so he was swapping the uncertain life of an advocate for a steadier role on the bench. In the Borders he soon became known as "The Shirra", Sheriff in the local dialect.

Scott's writing was taking up more and more of his time. Following their first publishing venture, he asked James Ballantyne to print his book of border ballads. Ballantyne agreed and Walter recruited local friends to help collect the scraps of verse which he was so passionate about preserving. They included John Leyden, the son of a Roxburghshire shepherd, who studied divinity at St Andrews University and loved the folklore and ballads of his native borders. Another of the collectors was James Hogg, a shepherd from the Ettrick valley who would go on to make a name for himself as a poet in his own right.

The Minstrelsy of the Scottish Border was published in 1802. It was met with wide acclaim but not everybody was a fan. James Hogg's mother was highly critical, telling Walter that as far as the ballads were concerned "you have spoilt them awthegither. They were made for singin' and no' for readin' but ye have broken the charm now an' they'll never be sung mair."

Despite Mrs Hogg's misgivings, the book quickly went into a second edition. By then Walter had started to write a ballad of his own, *The Lay of the Last Minstrel*, in response to a request from the Countess of Dalkeith to create a ballad about a mysterious goblin, Gilpin Horner, who was a legend in the area.

The completed piece, six cantos long, tells of an ageing minstrel who repays the hospitality of the Duchess of Buccleuch by telling her and her ladies the tale of a deadly sixteenth-century feud between two prominent Border clans, the Scotts and the Kerrs. Walter finished the first canto while he was laid up in a Musselburgh lodging, recovering from being kicked by a trooper's horse.

In 1804 Walter took a lease on the house of Ashestiel, near Clovenfords, four miles west of Galashiels. It was important that the Sheriff Depute live in the area he covered, and it was convenient for both Edinburgh and Selkirk, although the journey would have been at least five hours. He had inherited a house on the eastern edge of Kelso from his uncle, Captain Robert Scott and Walter would probably have preferred to live there. However, in those days when travel was by horse and carriage it was just too far out of the way for his work, so he sold it, hoping the proceeds would give him enough money to buy the kind of house he wanted to live in, in the right position surrounded by sufficient lands. Ashestiel was not for sale, it belonged to a relative who was living in India at the time, but it was a good stopgap in the Scotts' search for the perfect home.

Sophia had been joined by a brother, Walter, in October 1801, and then a sister, Anne, in February 1803. On Christmas Eve 1805 the last of the four children, Charles, was born at Ashesteil.

Walter was now in a well-paid job with a strong financial position so, buoyed up by the success of his books, he decided to invest in James Ballantyne's printing business which he ran with his brother John. James remained one of Walter's closest friends, and Walter appreciated the support he had offered in publishing the little book *An Apology for Tales of Terror* and the ballad *The Eve of St John* back in 1799. Walter believed that the risks were small, and the profits certain.

So confident of the investment was he that Walter persuaded the Ballantyne brothers to move from Kelso up to Edinburgh and to expand their business. But that confidence proved to be ill-placed. The Ballantynes might have been expert printers, but they had little business sense. Unaware of this, Walter left them to it. It was a decision that would come back to haunt him.

In early 1804, Walter and Charlotte paid a visit to the poet William Wordsworth at Grasmere. On their way home the couple stopped for a few romantic days at Gilsland where they first met. There, word reached them that the French had landed near Berwick and a large force of Volunteers was gathering at Dalkeith to see them off. Walter did not hesitate. He had accompanied his wife's carriage on horseback and immediately galloped north, covering the 100 miles in 24 hours to join his regiment, his head full of the drama of the news, and the danger to the country. In fact it was a false alarm, caused by charcoal burners near Berwick failing to dampen a fire. An eager sergeant at Hume Castle had mistaken the flames for one of the beacons which were to be lit to alert people to an invasion, and lit the Hume Castle beacon, which flashed the message across the borders and into Cumberland. Walter was delighted that the alarm system had worked, and that there was no invasion, so he turned and rode back to re-join his wife at Carlisle.

The following year *The Lay of the Last Minstrel* was published by Archibald Constable and Co, printed by the Ballantyne brothers. It immediately received excellent reviews. The Prime Minister, William Pitt, declared that "this is the sort of thing I might have expected in painting but could never have fancied capable of being given in poetry". In its first year 2250 copies were sold, making Walter Scott one of the most popular poets of the time.

Perversely, the success of *The Lay of the Last Minstrel* took its toll on the Ballantynes' business. They weren't prepared for the demand for reprints, and their lack of investment in equipment and materials over the years meant that cashflow problems nearly brought the business to its knees. Once again, Walter advanced the brothers money to help them survive the crisis. He and his publisher, Archibald Constable, had an uneasy relationship, which, in time, Walter would abandon in favour of a rival. Had he taken more advice from Constable at this early stage in his career, he might have avoided some of the financial stresses and strains that dominated so much of his later life.

CHAPTER SIX

In which Walter finds
success writing poetry,
and begins to create
his dream home.

Walter Scott described writing "as a good staff but a poor crutch". Like so many writers before and since he was all too aware that although he might enjoy the process, there was little money to be made from it, however accomplished he was. But the considerable success of *The Lay of the Last Minstrel* made him wonder, and he began to plan a future in which his writing, rather than the law, would provide the family's main living. He was enjoying the life of a Border laird with his family at Ashestiel and was more eager than ever to move to a larger house, shaped to his own taste, with its own estate.

Walter might have been tempted to abandon the living he was making in favour of writing, but he wasn't rash. He kept his strong links with the law and continued to excel in that world. In 1806 he succeeded George Hume of Wedderburn as the Clerk of the Court of Session, which kept him in close touch with his legal colleagues and a regular visitor to Edinburgh.

But Walter was happiest at home in Ashiesteil. He revelled in the company of his children. They were always welcome in his study, and he was never happier than when they demanded that he lay down his pen and tell them a story. As soon as they were old enough Walter would take them on his knee and tell them a legend or recite a ballad. Then he would set them down to carry on with their marbles or ninepins and return to his work refreshed.

He shared their joys and sorrows, and, always keen to excite their imaginations, told them stories about the history of their own country, often encouraging them to recite passages he chose for them by heart. Walter was always delighted when his daughters sang an old ditty or something of his own creation, and he made sure all his children learned to ride a horse.

Alongside their four children, Walter and Charlotte had an accumulation of the dogs which were to play a constant part in the family's life. A couple of greyhounds, Douglas and Percy, were followed by Camp the bull terrier, to whom Scott always spoke as though the dog was a wise old man. Many more, including his faithful hound Maida, a cross between a deerhound and a Pyrenean Mountain dog, were to follow over the years.

The household at Ashiesteil was supported by several loyal staff who were treated almost like members of the family. Tom Purdie had appeared before Walter at the Sherriff Court in Selkirk on a charge of poaching. He escaped a guilty verdict on a technicality, but Walter must have liked the look of him because he took him on first as a shepherd, and soon afterwards as his general factotum (an employee who does all kinds of work). Purdie was responsible for the house and grounds and Walter always appreciated his good, down-to-earth advice. Tom Purdie's brother-in-law, Peter Mathieson was the family's coachman. A good coachman was essential after Walter had caused his four wheeled phaeton to overturn several times with his wife on board. Other loyal retainers included John Macbeth the butler, Robert Hogg, the brother of James Hogg, the head shepherd, John of Skye the hedger, ditcher and personal piper, and John Nicholson the footman.

It was a happy household and on Sundays the family would walk for miles together, exploring the local area, just as Walter had done as a child.

Walter's literary horizons widened when he was commissioned by the London bookseller William Miller of Albemarle Street to gather a collection of the works of the pre-eminent Restoration poet and first Poet Laureate, John Dryden, whose work had long been neglected. He was to write notes about the poems and the poet himself. A commission like this was a sign of the esteem in which Walter was held, not just in Scotland. *"The Works of John Dryden, now first collected; illustrated with notes historical, critical and explanatory and a Life of the Author"* was published in 18 volumes in 1808 and, although several of his friends had doubted the wisdom of taking on the project, it was warmly received.

After this success, Walter wanted to get back to writing his own work. He decided to build on the success of *the Lay of the Last Minstrel* and planned another long ballad, this one leading to a final scene at the battlefield of Flodden – a battle in 1513 that had cast a long shadow. It had been Scotland's most devastating defeat, as a result of which the country lost its king, most of its leaders and a huge number of its men of fighting age, "the flowers of the forest". It was an event that left a mark on generations of Scottish families and Walter wanted to put words to that national grief.

Marmion was also published in 1808. A wild romance, it tells of the rich Clara de Clare who retires to a convent to avoid the unwelcome attentions of the disreputable Lord Marmion. He retaliates by falsely implicating Clara's fiancé, Sir Ralph De Wilton, in treason. The story, of course, has a happy ending.

With its fiery scenes of passion and combat, *Marmion* was an immediate best-seller, lifting people's spirits during the dark days of Napoleon's successes on the European continent. Its success also alarmed the publisher Archibald Constable, who, anxious not to lose an author who was making him substantial profits, offered Walter a handsome £1500 to write about the life of the Anglo-Irish poet and satirist Jonathan Swift, the author of *Gulliver's Travels* and Dean of St Patrick's Cathedral in Dublin. Walter accepted the commission, to Constable's relief, and, while he was researching the subject, he was spurred on to compose another great ballad.

Published in 1810, *The Lady of the Lake* has six cantos, each of which takes place over a single day. Set at the gateway to the Highlands of Scotland, the Trossachs, the story has three main strands: the contest among three men to win the love of Ellen Douglas; the feud and reconciliation of King James the Fifth of Scotland and the powerful James Douglas; and a war between the lowland Scots and the Highland clans.

These poems had a tremendous influence in the nineteenth century. Readers within Scotland revelled in such lavish tales of their own history. Those outwith the country were so swept away by the writing that many of them longed to visit Scotland. It is incredible that these same words continue to inspire people from all over the world. Each night, for thirty years, lines from *The Lay of the Last Minstrel* have rounded off the world-famous Royal Edinburgh Military Tattoo for its huge international audiences.

Breathes there the man, with soul so dead
Who never to himself hath said,
This is my own - my native land!
Land of brown heath and shaggy wood,
Land of the mountain and the flood,
Land of my sires! what mortal hand
Can e'er untie the filial band
That knits me to thy rugged strand?

Even the most sophisticated of advertising copywriters would fail to match Scott's description of the ruined Melrose Abbey:

If thou wouldst view fair Melrose aright,
Go visit it by the pale moonlight;
For the gay beams of lightsome day
Gild but to flout the ruins gray.

And it is little wonder that people were drawn to visit the landscape of the Trossachs, lured by such glorious descriptions as this, from *The Lady of the Lake*:

Each purple peak, each flinty spire
was bathed in floods of living fire

In fact, the area became so attractive to visitors that the politician, Sir John Sinclair, recorded a 200% increase in toll-payments for carriages.

More poetic ballads would follow but Scott was no fool. He was delighted by his success but aware that public taste can be fickle. He was a generous host, with ambitious expectations of life for him and his family, all of which required a good income. He also kept an eye on the competition in particular Lord Byron, whose popularity was growing at that time.

Byron had published the first couple of cantos of his long narrative poem, *Childe Harold's Pilgrimage*, in 1812. He immediately became the most dazzling star in Regency London. Byron's poem describes the travels of a young man training to be a knight, disillusioned with a life of pleasure and revelry who seeks distraction in foreign lands. The romance of the writing, like Walter Scott's, touched a public weary of Napoleon's wars and unsettled by a monarch, George III, who was considered unfit to rule.

Byron's success kept Walter on his toes. Having looked around for subjects to inspire his next major work, Walter decided to celebrate the recent victories of the Duke of Wellington against Napoleon's forces in Spain and Portugal. *The Vision of Don Roderick* was based on an account by the Spanish poet Ginés Pérez de Hita of the legendary consultation of an oracle by the last Visigoth King of Spain, around the year 711. The vision, showed the country's conquest by the Moors, the Spanish Inquisition, the assault by Napoleon and finally the triumphant arrival of British forces to liberate the country. Walter chose to give the profits from this poem to support military veterans who had suffered in the campaigns in Portugal.

Next Scott began work on another romantic poem, this one set in the age of Cavaliers and Roundheads during the English Civil War in the 17th century. Rokeby – published by the Ballantynes - was a deliberate move to broaden his appeal to readers south of the border. Rokeby Park in Teesdale belonged to Scott's friend, the antiquary and MP, John Bacon Sawrey Morritt. Scott had decided that the area was sadly lacking in legends, so he set out to redress this balance with a tale of love and villainy, and although the poem was not as successful as he had hoped, overshadowed by Byron's fantastically popular *Childe Harold's Pilgrimage*, it still sold thousands of copies and several dozen songs and musical adaptations were derived from it.

Walter was never short of ideas. As soon as *Rokeby* was finished, he began a poetic fantasy based on the story of Sleeping Beauty. *The Bridal of Triermain* is set in Cumberland where the hero, Sir Roland De Vaux, embarked on a quest to revive Gyneth, daughter of King Arthur, doomed by the wizard Merlin to an enchanted sleep inside a magic castle 500 years previously.

It was while he was writing *The Bridal of Triermain* that he was told that the lease on Ashestiel was coming to an end. The pressure was on. Although they had bought a town house in Edinburgh – 38 North Castle Street - in 1802, Walter and Charlotte needed a permanent home for their family in their beloved Scottish Borders, and Walter had a clear idea of what that might be. It was a surprise, then, when he took his family to see a small, rather unimpressive farm named Cartley Hole belonging to the minister of Galashiels. The land had been the site of the last battle between the Scott and the Kerr clans in 1526 and had once belonged to Melrose Abbey, both facts that would not have been lost on Walter.

The farmhouse sat on a shelf of rising ground, its only redeeming feature being the River Tweed that flowed below it. But Scott was confident that it would provide him with the home he needed, and, in the spring of 1812, he and his family left Ashestiel and crossed the Tweed with 24 cartloads of what he called "the veriest trash in nature besides dogs, pigs, poultry, cows, calves, bareheaded wenches and bare breeched boys" as well as "old swords, targets and lances. A family of turkeys was accommodated in the helmet of some preux chevalier (gallant knight) of ancient Border fame". They were accompanied by dozens of local children carrying fishing rods and spears and leading ponies, greyhounds, and spaniels. The departure of the Scott family from Ashiesteil must have been quite a sight.

Chapter Seven

In which Walter
writes his first
novel, the first
of many!

The family's leaving was much lamented around Ashestiel. Both Walter and Charlotte were well known members of the local community, particularly active in supplying medical advice when it was needed to the scattered cottagers of the district. Charlotte had often gone out of her way to visit the sick and disperse the contents of her medicine chest, along with the contents of her larder and cellar.

Contained amongst the 24 cartloads, was a collection of all sorts of odd things randomly amassed by Walter since his early childhood. It included armour, cuirasses, helmets, stirrups, spurs, claymores, chain mail, even Rob Roy's gun. Later he added Napoleon Bonaparte's pistols. Soon after they moved in, Walter renamed Cartley Hole, Abbotsford and began to plan its renovation. In time, that vast and eclectic collection would go on display there.

The strength of Walter's reputation could not have been clearer than when he was offered the post of Poet Laureate in 1813. The holder of this long-standing honorary position, appointed by the King or Queen of the time, would be expected to write verses for significant national occasions. Perhaps it was a sign that Walter's mind was already leaving poetry behind when he refused the invitation, writing in his reply that he would "always consider it as the proudest incident of my life".

Walter had decided that in order to build on his success, he must begin to tell his stories in prose. *Rokeby* had not done badly, but it had not done as well as he had hoped, and Walter was concerned that he might be losing the public's favour. He even tried to persuade a friend to put his name to *The Bridal of Triermain* and when that failed, he published it anonymously.

But Walter was busy in every aspect of his life. He had great plans for his new home. He hired an architect to design extensions and frontages to completely remodel the original farmhouse and soon, masons were busily transforming the rather ordinary little farmhouse into something much grander. Encouraged when he saw his original plans taking shape, Scott's ambitions for the place grew, but they did not come cheap. Despite the financial implications, he could not resist buying more land or adding to his collection of random artefacts.

The 19 volumes of his *Life of Swift*, which had been commissioned in 1808, appeared in July 1814 to general approval. Scott had included many "admirable pieces both in prose and verse" which had escaped notice among the many old pamphlets and broadsides, overshadowed by Dean Jonathan Swift's better-known works. Swift had made a fascinating subject; the biographical part of the work showed "an intimacy of acquaintance with the obscurest details of the political, social and literary history of the period of Queen Anne".

Walter was glad of the good reviews, but his writing ambitions took him beyond the role of editor. He had his heart set on writing more stories, inspired by the history and geography of Scotland.

One day a friend came to visit Abbotsford when the

salmon were running in the Tweed. Walter had gone rummaging through the drawers of an old cabinet to find extra fishing tackle for him and came across a manuscript he had abandoned some time earlier. It was the start of a novel. Walter placed the pages on his desk as he went back to join his friend on the river. It was a sign. All he need do was set to work and finish it.

The novel he had started was set at the time of the 1745 Jacobite uprising and viewed lowland and highland Scots through the eyes of an educated English soldier. Walter called it *Waverley* after the hero of the book, and the books which followed became known as the Waverley novels.

Walter set to work with renewed vigour and the novel was published in Edinburgh in 1814 in three volumes under its full title - *WAVERLEY* or *'Tis Sixty Years Since* - without the author's name on it. The decision to publish anonymously was not surprising, as novel writing then was not held in the high regard that it is today. When Walter wrote *Waverley*, it would have been considered inappropriate for a judge or a clerk of the court to be caught writing fiction. He was also afraid that the public might think that it had already heard quite enough of Walter Scott.

Soon Edinburgh was buzzing with rumours about who this new author could be. As the speculation grew, Walter went to great trouble to divert attention away from himself. "I shall whistle it down the wind and let it prey at fortune." It was a shrewd tactic, and he was aware that the mystery of the novel's authorship was actually increasing sales.

Over the years it became an open secret that *Waverley* had been written by Walter Scott, but it wasn't until 1827 that he publicly acknowledged that fact.

Walter had worked very hard and extraordinarily fast to complete his manuscript, a fact that was reflected in a story told by his future son-in-law, John Gibson Lockhart. Sometime in the months before Waverley was published, a young advocate, William Menzies, had invited some of his friends to dinner, gathering afterwards in the library of the Menzies' house in George Street in Edinburgh. It had a window looking north at right angles to North Castle Street. Sitting there, Menzies' behaviour suddenly changed. He became very anxious and jittery, and begged to change places with Lockhart, "for there is a confounded hand in sight of me here which has often bothered me before. I have been watching it, it fascinated my eye, it never stops, page after page is finished and thrown on that heap of manuscripts and still it goes on unwearied, and so it will be until candles are brought in and God knows how long after that. It is the same every night, I can't stand a sight of it when I am not at my books."

Lockhart and the other guests were mystified by Menzies' strange reaction, and tried to calm him down, insisting it must be "some stupid, dogged clerk". But Menzies' father settled the matter for them, saying, "No, boys. I well know what hand it is, 'tis Walter Scott's".

Waverley, widely credited with being one of the world's first historical novels, was astonishingly successful but Scott did not wait around to find that out. Instead, in the

July of 1814, he embarked on an extended tour of the Scottish islands. He was a passenger on board the Lighthouse Yacht with the Commissioners of the Northern Lights under the Surveyor-Viceroy, Mr Robert Stevenson, grandfather of the writer Robert Louis Stevenson.

The cruise took him away from the clacking tongues in Edinburgh, up to Orkney and Shetland and through the Pentland Firth to the Western Isles, where he gathered descriptions of the landscape he needed for his next work before they sailed round to the north coast of Ulster and back to Scotland. It was only then that Walter learned how well *Waverley* had been received.

Perhaps the astonishing success of *Waverley* spurred Walter on. The truth was that he never lacked the motivation to write. He was already adept at juggling several literary works at a time and in January 1815 he published a new ballad, *The Lord of the Isles*, with Walter Scott credited as the author this time. The ballad tells of the exile of King Robert the Bruce and his return to victory at the Battle of Bannockburn. It was well received by the critics but not as well by the public. Walter accepted their judgement with good-humoured resignation; he was already working on something new.

Walter claimed that his second novel, *Guy Mannering*, took six weeks to write over Christmas. It appeared two months after The Lord of the Isles and introduced some of his best loved characters in the wild gypsy Meg Merrilees, the Liddesdale farmer Dandie Dinmont and the Dutch smuggler Dirk Hatteraick. Instead of the author's name, the new book was simply inscribed "By The Author Of Waverley" on the title page.

Scott was, by this time, short of funds and in publishing more books, he saw a way to ease the financial pressures. His grandiose plans for Abbotsford did not come cheap, compounded by his generosity to needy friends, and his continued support for the Ballantyne Printers. He completed another novel, *The Antiquary*, in four months. It is set in north-east Scotland in the last decade of the 18th century and evoked the nationwide fear of a French invasion and Republican insurrection with its theme of the influence of the past on the present. Of all his prose works this was the one Scott liked best.

Unfortunately, it was not the bestseller he had hoped for, so he pressed on with a new idea for a series of five stories to be called *Tales of my Landlord*. The second of these, *Old Mortality*, was the most successful, and is now regarded as an accomplished evocation of the atmosphere of Scotland in the 17th Century. 'Old Mortality', Robert Paterson, decides to travel around Scotland re-engraving the tombs of Covenanter martyrs. The tale describes Robert Paterson's anecdotes and other stories of the times to present a rounded picture of the age.

By now, Scott was nearing middle age. He was widely acknowledged not just as the country's finest storyteller but also as the most famous living man in Scotland. Although the novels were published anonymously, his authorship of them was an open secret. That success had come at the price of his legal career, Scott would have liked a promotion from his position as Clerk to the Court of Session to an appointment as a judge. It was not so much a career ambition as a desire to take life a little easier, but the promotion was not forthcoming.

Scott was not a well man. His odd life, one half of which was spent sitting in cramped, stuffy court rooms, the other half in the hard physical exertion of his long walks and rides, had caught up with him. He enjoyed food and with it went quite a lot of drinking of wine and whisky punch. He rarely had enough sleep and he often forgot to change out of his wet clothes after walks in the border countryside. An attack from gallstones in 1817 certainly didn't help. His doctors prescribed various remedies but failed to deal properly with the painful problem for another three years.

Yet Scott refused to slow down, insisting on keeping on with his energetic life, expanding his estate and writing more anonymous *Waverley* novels. It was not in his personality to relax the pace at which he lived his life, but the considerable financial pressures remained.

The highland hero, Rob Roy, had long been in Scott's mind as the subject for a novel. Alexander Stewart had told him of his broadsword duel with Rob Roy Macgregor, and *The Lady of the Lake* had drawn him to the place where the outlaw was born. The novel contrasted the standards of the Scottish highlanders with those of the rest of the country and introduced such memorable characters as Rob Roy himself and his unforgiving wife Helen, the shrewd Glasgow merchant Bailie Nicol Jarvie, the gentle Diana Vernon and the cunning and indifferently loyal servant Andrew Fairservice. The novel was an instant best-seller. The first printing of 10,000 copies sold out in two weeks and with the money Walter received he was able to clear more of the debt remaining from the Ballantyne venture and pay for the extravagant additions to his estate.

Although he remained the Sheriff Depute in Selkirk and Clerk of the Court of Session, the success of *Rob Roy* ensured that writing was now Walter Scott's main occupation.

But his reputation as a public figure was building too, offering Walter dazzling opportunities to make his mark in other ways.

CHAPTER
EIGHT

In which Walter
is tasked with finding
the Scottish Crown
Jewels.

The Scots had insisted that Charles the First was crowned with the old Scottish regalia, known as the Honours of Scotland, at the Palace of Holyroodhouse in Edinburgh in 1633, following his coronation at Westminster Abbey in 1626, amidst the most magnificent pageantry Scotland had ever seen. His son, Charles the Second, was crowned in more modest circumstances at Scone on New Year's Day 1651 and shortly afterwards the regalia, the Crown, the Sceptre, and the Sword of State, were removed to Dunnottar Castle on the north-east coast of Scotland and all but forgotten.

But Oliver Cromwell had not forgotten. He had already ensured that the Crown Jewels of England were broken up and sold off. Now his army was hurrying north to do the same to the Scottish regalia. A plan was hatched to smuggle the precious objects out of the castle to the small parish church of Kinneff four or five miles away. There the Crown and the Sceptre were buried in a hole under the floor of the church just in front of the pulpit, and the Sword of State under the floor at the back of the church.

When the Governor surrendered Dunnottar Castle, Cromwell's men were furious to discover the regalia gone. They were told repeatedly that the precious objects had been taken to Paris and despite some rough treatment of the Governor and his lady, the secret of their whereabouts was never revealed. When King Charles was restored to the throne in 1660 the Honours of Scotland miraculously reappeared and were used regularly in the sittings of the Scottish Parliament until 1707 when the Parliaments of Scotland and England were dissolved.

When the single Parliament for Great Britain was formed, many in Scotland feared that the Honours would be removed to London, so they were deposited for safekeeping in a strong oak chest secured by three heavy padlocks, in the Crown Room of Edinburgh Castle. The Jacobites, unhappy at the union with England, spread fake rumours that the regalia had gone. Tales of their loss continued to circulate down the years.

Keen to solve the mystery of the Honours of Scotland, Walter began pressing the Prince Regent to allow the Crown Room to be opened and the contents of the great oak chest to be revealed. His persistence paid off. On 4th February 1818, a group of nine eminent men, including senior law officers, the Lord Provost of Edinburgh and Walter Scott gathered at the Crown Room only to discover that the keys to the padlocks had been lost.

The gentlemen watched anxiously as a hurriedly summoned blacksmith named Neish laboured to force open the chest. Not all of them were confident they would find what they were looking for but when the lid was finally raised, there, wrapped in linen, were the Honours of Scotland and more besides.

Along with the Crown of Robert the Bruce were the Sceptre and the Sword of State plus the Lord High Treasurer of Scotland's Mace of Office, the badge and collar of the Order of the Garter, the Coronation ring of King Charles the First and a badge of St Andrew containing a miniature of Anne of Denmark, the Queen of King James the Sixth.

The event caught the imagination of the people of Edinburgh. Crowds had been gathering, waiting on the Castlehill for news. Walter Scott had been proved right in his judgement that the ancient Scottish regalia had been secure in the Castle for all those years and that the time was right for them to be safely revealed. The Honours, which were in remarkably good condition, were put on display in the Castle in 1819 and to add to the drama of it all, the guards were kitted out in the dress of the Bodyguards of the ancient Kings of Scotland.

His part in the return of the Honours of Scotland to public view made Walter an even more popular figure in the country. His fortunes seemed to be improving after some difficult years. He was offered a baronetcy towards the end of 1818, and he accepted it with great pride. He was now Sir Walter Scott.

His health continued to trouble him however, and he struggled with long bouts of pain and sickness. His friend the Duke of Buccleuch died in 1819 and at the time, the seriously ill Scott must have believed he would not be long behind him. Around that time his future son-in-law John Gibson Lockhart wrote "his countenance was meagre, haggard and of the deadliest yellow of the jaundice and his hair, which a few weeks before had been but slightly sprinkled with grey, was now almost literally snow white."

Stubbornly determined, Scott rallied and tried to resume his activities but during the second half of 1819 he relapsed. Thinking the end was near, his children were called to his bedside. As his daughter Sophie recalled, "he gave each one such advice as suited their years and characters" and added, "For myself, my dears, I am unconscious of ever having done any man an injury or omitted any fair opportunity of doing any man a benefit." Then he laid his hand on their heads and blessed them. But he did not die. Instead, he fell into a deep sleep and amazingly began to recover.

Apart from the good care of his family, there can be no doubt that Scott's strength of character pulled him through this critical illness and despite his agonies, he went on writing.

He completed another story for *Tales of my Landlord*, *Heart of Midlothian*. He had planned two stories but this one, now regarded as Scott's finest, grew and grew until it became one novel. He set it in Edinburgh during the time of the Porteous Riots in 1736 when a mob killed Captain John Porteous of the City Guard after he had ordered his men to fire into a riotous crowd, killing several of them. The novel relates what had essentially been a true story of the virtuous Jeanie Deans, who walked to London to seek clemency from Queen Caroline for her younger sister, Effie, who had been accused of killing her infant.

The tale was based on the true story of Helen Walker from Irongray who had walked the 300 miles to London to obtain a pardon for her sister Isabella. Sir Walter had learned the story from a Mrs Goldie in Dumfries and borrowed it for his character of Jeanie Deans. With typical generosity, after *Heart of Midlothian* was published, Sir

Walter had a handsome monument built for the grave where Miss Walker was buried in Irongray Churchyard.

Because Sir Walter was too weak to write, he dictated *The Bride of Lammermoor*, a tragic love story which descends into deception and madness, while he lay on his sofa. His scribes were William Laidlaw and John Ballantyne. Sir Walter preferred John Ballantyne for the job as he always came prepared with a dozen pens and could write quickly without pausing. In contrast, William Laidlaw, the steward at Abbotsford, kept exclaiming and commenting throughout the dictation.

The Bride of Lammermoor was coupled with *A Legend of Montrose*, which was loosely based on a murder after the battle of Tippermuir. It was well received but languished in the shadow of the previous novel.

When he was presented with a printed copy, Walter found that he could not remember any of the incidents or characters he had dictated through his illness. Rather like Samuel Taylor Coleridge who composed *Kubla Khan* under the influence of opium, Scott had been carried into a strange world by the medicines he was prescribed. The novels he wrote during the years of his illness reflect a novelist at the peak of his powers.

Walter had always been intrigued by the Middle Ages, especially the period from the 12th to the 15th centuries. While he was ill, he had started to dictate a tale which dipped deep into this period of history in the stirring, romantic tale of *Ivanhoe*, published at the end of 1819.

After publishing a series of stories set in Scotland, it was a shrewd and calculated move to now appeal to his readers in England, with a rattling good tale introducing more than 150 characters, including Richard the Lionheart and that astonishingly skilful archer Robin Hood.

The publication of *Ivanhoe*, in John Gibson Lockhart's opinion, marked "the most brilliant epoch in Scott's history as the literary favourite of his contemporaries."

But the triumph of publication was overshadowed by personal loss. Walter's mother, who had been ailing for only a couple of weeks, died on Christmas Eve 1819. Her brother and sister had died barely a week earlier.

Sir Walter was also all too aware of social turmoil, locally and nationally. The miners of Northumberland and the weavers of the West of Scotland, encouraged by the revolutions in France and America, colluded to create unrest in what became known as the Radical War. The weavers of the Borders refused to join them and made their loyalty known to the Shirra. Much of Walter's time was taken up in helping to organise a new levy of volunteers known as the Buccleuch Legion who were prepared to march to the English border to turn back any trouble.

But there was happiness too. His elder daughter Sophia became engaged to John Gibson Lockhart in February 1820, and they were married at Abbotsford three months later.

In March Sir Walter set off for London where King George

the Fourth conferred his baronetcy personally and when "the great unknown", as the author was often referred to, had kissed his hand, His Majesty said to him, "I shall always reflect with pleasure on Sir Walter Scott's having been the first creation of my reign."

Scott also sat for a portrait by Sir Thomas Lawrence commissioned by the King for the great gallery at Windsor and he gave sittings for the best-known bust of him by the sculptor Francis Chantry. Sir Walter's next novel, *The Monastery*, had been started before *Ivanhoe* and was one of his *Tales from Benedictine Sources*. It appeared at the beginning of March 1820 and although many reviewers found it disappointing after *Ivanhoe*, citing the author's exhaustion and haste, they were far from being universally negative. Sir Walter had already embarked on a sequel, *The Abbot*, published later in 1820, which was inspired by the imprisonment, escape and defeat of Mary Queen of Scots in Loch Leven Castle in 1567. Woven throughout was the romance of the dim-witted but spirited Roland Graeme.

In contrast to *The Monastery*, reviewers generally welcomed *The Abbot* as a return to form, several commenting favourably on the author's even-handed treatment of the religious divide of the time.

Kenilworth, which Scott's biographer John Buchan called his "masterpiece in sheer craftsmanship", was published at the start of 1821. It was filled with a glittering cast of historical characters and figures drawn from local stories in Warwickshire and tells the tragic story of the secret marriage of Robert Dudley, the Earl of Leicester, to Amy

Robsart. The weak and ambitious Earl kept the marriage secret while he courted the favour of Queen Elizabeth to help him rise to power. The Queen uncovers the truth and shames the Earl, but sadly too late to save Amy who has been murdered by Dudley's steward.

Nearing fifty, Walter was finally enjoying better health and revelling in the success of his books. While Charlotte managed the house with care, their family was growing up and starting their own lives. Sophia had given birth to a son, and their elder son Walter had transferred to the 15th King's Hussars with a commission as a lieutenant. Charles was preparing to go to Oxford University, and Walter and Charlotte had the comfort of their younger daughter Anne who remained at home where she would nurse her mother and later her father in their final years.

In the summer of 1821 Sir Walter travelled to London for the Coronation of King George the Fourth. While he was in the city, he was preoccupied with the completion of his beloved Abbotsford, writing to Charlotte that he thought there should be "a handsome library and you with a drawing room and better bedroom. It will cost me a little hard work to meet the expense, but I have been a good while idle."

By now Sir Walter felt himself fully recovered. His book sales were going from strength to strength and any other man of his age might have taken some time to reflect and enjoy that success. But Sir Walter's restless mind was already turning to a grand idea which was to seal his influence on Scottish life for generations to come.

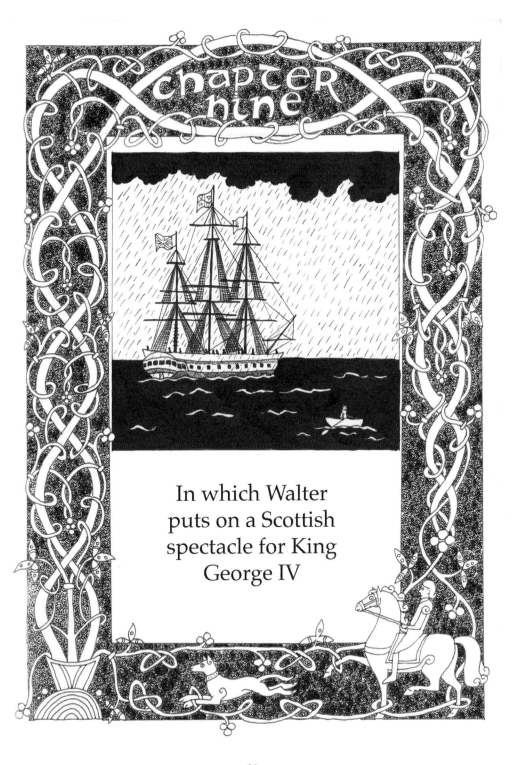

CHAPTER nine

In which Walter
puts on a Scottish
spectacle for King
George IV

Sir Walter Scott worked steadily, writing for around three or four hours each day, usually in the early morning before breakfast when he would be undisturbed. He had a talent for closing his mind to what was going on around him; whether he was sitting as a Sheriff or a Clerk, listening to advocates droning on, or whether he was out in his estate at Abbotsford, Scott would be constantly thinking of the novel he had in hand.

Kenilworth was followed fairly swiftly by *The Pirate*, a curious tale set in Shetland, which Walter had visited in 1814 aboard the Lighthouse Yacht. It was loosely based on the life of the notorious pirate John Gow who was hanged in 1725. The novel tells the story of the complicated romantic lives of two sisters, Minna and Brenda Troil and a man called Mordaunt Mertoun. The latter rescues a shipwrecked Captain called Clement Cleveland, who turns out to have been a pirate. The two men are revealed to be brothers and, in the end, unlike John Gow, Cleveland dies an honourable and gallant death in government service.

No sooner had Walter finished *The Pirate* than he was already busy on *The Fortunes of Nigel*, in which a young Scottish nobleman, Nigel Olifaunt (Lord Glenvarloch), travels to London to ask King James the Sixth and First for the repayment of a loan from his father. Nigel, hopelessly unsophisticated and unaware of just how nasty the intrigues of Court life could be, soon finds himself in mortal danger. Among the colourful characters in the story, Scott draws a sympathetic portrait of the Edinburgh goldsmith George "Jingling Geordie" Heriot, who is persuaded to pay for Nigel's wedding feast, and who in real life left a lasting mark on Edinburgh by founding George Heriot's Hospital, now George Heriot's School.

Then, in 1822 everything changed. The newly crowned King George the Fourth decided to visit Scotland. And he needed local, respected help if he was going to make a success of it.

The timing of this visit was entirely political. The British Government wanted to keep the King well clear of the Congress of Verona, an international gathering to settle the balance of power in Europe after the fall of Napoleon seven years earlier. So, to make sure he was unable to interfere, his courtiers decided that this would be the perfect time for him to make a state visit to Scotland, the first by a British monarch since King Charles the Second for his coronation in 1651.

But the new king was widely unpopular among the Scots. Many of them were offended by his appalling treatment of his late wife, Caroline, whom he hated and would not allow to become Queen. She, on the other hand, had been wildly popular with the British people.

The courtiers were in a quandary. The Scots were unlikely to welcome their badly-behaved King with open arms. They required local expertise, somebody respected who could handle themselves, and the King. They cast about for individuals of sufficient reputation who might manage the royal visit. In the end, there was only one possible choice. The one man capable of organising such a Royal visit, and making a success of it, was Sir Walter Scott.

A staunch Royalist, and ever the great romantic, Sir Walter saw this as a wonderful opportunity to rebrand the unpopular monarch in the mould of Bonnie Prince Charlie. Even before the days of social media and wall-to-wall television coverage, it was vital that George IV looked the part. As a Stuart prince and a Jacobite highlander, Sir Walter declared that the king was properly entitled to wear the kilt and set about ensuring that he would wear it well. As a result, the King spent what in today's money would have been about £120,000 on a bright red highland outfit, using some 100 metres of satin, velvet and cashmere, bearing the tartan now known as Royal Stewart. This included a military style red tunic, an elaborate goatskin sporran with a massive gold top, appropriately diced hose and buckled slippers, and a bonnet "consisting of the Royal Scots crown in miniature set with diamonds, pearls, rubies and emeralds". All of this was accessorised with gold chains, a dirk, a sword, and a set of pistols.

At that time, the Palace of Holyroodhouse was too run-down to be a royal residence, so it was decided that the King would stay at the young Duke of Buccleuch's residence, Dalkeith Palace, on the outskirts of Edinburgh. Sir Walter was determined that the entire visit would be one long lavish production, a crowd-pleaser on a scale the nation had never known before, and he drew on the advice of his friend the young actor-manager William Henry Murray whose talents at creating scenery and costume were put to superb use.

Sir Walter left as little as possible to chance, going so far as to publish, and sell for a shilling, "HINTS addressed to the INHABITANTS OF EDINBURGH AND OTHERS in prospect of HIS MAJESTY'S VISIT. By an old citizen". The booklet gave an outline of the events planned, with detailed advice on behaviour and dress. However, not everybody approved. The Highland chiefs were especially touchy, unused to being told what to do, but Sir Walter was adamant. Failure was not an option.

The first of the pageants took place on Monday 12 August 1822, the King's 60th birthday. The Midlothian Yeomanry and companies of Highlanders escorted the coaches carrying the Regalia of Scotland and dignitaries from Edinburgh Castle to Holyroodhouse in preparation for the King's arrival.

Two days later, around noon on Wednesday 14th August, the King's yacht "HMY Royal George" arrived in the Firth of Forth. It was raining so heavily that the King decided to delay his landing until the next day. But Sir Walter was undeterred by bad weather, and he was rowed out to see the King, who rewarded him by exclaiming "What! Sir Walter Scott, the man in Scotland I most wish to see!"

After a toast in whisky, Scott presented to the King a gift, a silver St Andrews Cross embroidered with pearls on blue velvet designed and embroidered by the Ladies of Edinburgh. Around it was a belt of gold with a diamond buckle and magnificent Scottish pearls surmounted by the imperial crown picked out in diamonds, rubies, emeralds and topaz. Inscribed on the cross was: "Righ Albainn gu brath", Gaelic for "Long life to the King of Scotland". The

King promised to wear it in public. As a memento, Scott asked for the King's whisky glass which was carefully wrapped up and stowed in what he thought was his safest pocket.

When he returned home, he found the English poet George Crabbe waiting for him, keen to find out how the day had gone. Scott threw himself into his chair, delighted that the day had gone as well as it had and glad to share the news of it all with his friend only to hear the ominous crack of breaking glass as the precious royal keepsake shattered in his pocket.

The next day the King arrived in sunshine at the quayside of The Shore at Leith and stepped onto a red carpet, strewn with flowers, to greet the waiting crowds. He was met by a guard of more than fifty members of the Royal Company of Archers - the monarch's bodyguard in Scotland - to which Sir Walter had been elected the previous year.

An enormous procession, headed by three trumpeters from the Midlothian Yeomanry Cavalry, followed by mounted cavalrymen, pipers, numerous highlanders, law officers and members of the Royal Household, preceded the open royal carriage carrying the King with the bodyguard of Archers marching alongside. Scott's son-in-law, John Gibson Lockhart described the scene, "Lines of tents, flags and artillery circled Arthur's Seat, Salisbury Crags and the Calton Hill". The Castle and its rock were "wreathed in the smoke of repeated salvoes while a huge royal banner, such as had not waved since 1745, floated and flapped over all."

The cavalcade passed cheering crowds all the way to the top of Leith Walk, where it was formally admitted to the City at a theatrical "medieval" gateway. The keys to the city were presented to the king, while a huge crowd on Calton Hill sang the National Anthem. Such a positive reception was something that would have seemed out of the question only a few months before. The procession continued on to the Palace of Holyroodhouse where it was received by a second guard of honour from the Royal Company of Archers, led by the Captain General, the Earl of Hopetoun. Inside, the King was presented with the Keys to the palace and a pair of silver headed barbed arrows on a green velvet cushion. This "reddendo" was a royal tribute laid down in the Royal Company of Archers charter, dating from the time of Queen Anne in 1704.

The King then retired to Dalkeith Palace for a rest, returning to Edinburgh the following evening to look at the illuminations and illustrated tributes. On the afternoon of Saturday 17 August, the great and good queued at Holyrood to get a closer look at their monarch on the only occasion on which he wore his wildly expensive kilt. Despite the cost, it wasn't a perfect fit. King George's legs were covered in "buff coloured trowsers like flesh to imitate his Royal knees". When someone complained that the kilt had been too short for modesty, Lady Hamilton -Dalrymple wittily responded, "Since he is to be among us for so short a time, the more we see of him the better."

On the afternoon of Monday the 19th, the King went in to Holyroodhouse to listen to a series of addresses from the Church of Scotland, the Scottish Episcopal Church, universities, burghs, counties, and the Highland Society, and to make his short, formal responses. It probably wasn't the most riveting of occasions for any of those present, but a necessary part of any royal visit.

The King's Drawing Room at Holyrood on the next afternoon was attended by a throng of nearly 500 richly dressed ladies, most bearing coloured ostrich plumes above their elaborately curled hair. Custom required that the courteous and smiling King kiss each one on the cheek. In such a crush some either received no kiss or did not remember feeling the royal lips. Lady Scott and her daughters Sophia and Anne were among the lucky ones.

After a quiet day at Dalkeith, the Grand Procession from Holyrood to Edinburgh Castle on Thursday 22 August took place despite heavy rain. This was a recreation of the old custom of the "Riding of the Parliament" when processions rode from Holyrood up to Parliament Hall, behind St Giles Cathedral. The procession and the King's closed carriage proceeded slowly up the Royal Mile flanked by colourful bunting and densely packed, cheering crowds obscured by their umbrellas. The windows and the balconies along the length of the street were all covered with green and scarlet cloth.

At one o'clock the different public bodies, incorporations, and trades took the places assigned to them, with crosses on their breasts, heather or thistles in their hats, most of them holding white rods in their hands. The society of gardeners displayed a floral triple feather, remembering the years the King had spent as Prince of Wales, and the officer of the society of glassblowers wore a glass hat, with a glass sword and target, each of his members carrying a long glass rod.

The important dignitaries dressed in magnificent costumes rode on horseback but Sir Walter, dressed in the Windsor uniform, a type of formal dress worn at Windsor Castle only by members of the royal family and very senior courtiers, walked up the centre of the street along with two other gentlemen and was loudly cheered all the way.

When the King's carriage reached the Castle, he dismounted and was presented with the keys by the Governor, Lieutenant-General Sir Alexander Hope, before he walked over the drawbridge where another carriage took him up to the half-moon battery. There, in the rain, he mounted a platform in full view of his admiring subjects. A royal salute was fired from the guns on the ramparts, the bands played 'God Save the King', and the soldiers presented arms. The King stayed on the platform for at least 15 minutes, cheered by the multitude who had gathered on the Castle-hill.

One of his attendants was worried that the King would get wet. "O, never mind," replied his Majesty, "I must cheer the people" and taking off his hat, he waved it repeatedly and loudly gave three cheers. The weather didn't let up, but it seemed not to have dampened the enthusiasm of either the crowds or the King. Instead, it added a wild and romantic effect, with the broken outlines of crags and cliffs and the city's buildings, emerging through the mist. The crowd made the air resound with repeated acclamations and the King exclaimed, "This is wonderful! What a fine sight! I had no conception there was such a fine scene in the world; and to find it in my own dominions; and the people are as beautiful and as extraordinary as the scene." He was not accustomed to this kind of reception.

The following day, 3,000 volunteer cavalrymen formed up on Portobello sands for the King's inspection during which he was also to honour the Clans, including a contingent from the Celtic Society of Edinburgh. Although his review ended before he reached them, the Highlanders took part in the Grand March Past and were cheered enthusiastically by the crowds as they marched back to Edinburgh.

In the evening, Sir Walter had organised a Highland Ball. The much sought-after invitation had thrown many lowland gentlemen into a state of confusion as they hastily embarked on a desperate search for Highland ancestry and an appropriate kilt from the Edinburgh tailors. Working round the clock to meet the demand, they responded with a creative flair for finding or inventing something suitable. This was the society event which established tartan and kilts as the national dress of Scotland.

The Assembly Rooms had been theatrically transformed by William Henry Murray for the occasion. Instead of his kilt, King George appeared wearing his Field Marshal's uniform, however he thoroughly enjoyed watching the kilted dancers whirl through their reels and strathspeys. He had made it clear that while he was in Scotland, all music should be "purely national and characteristic" and Sir Walter ensured that those instructions were followed to the last note. The King may have left before midnight, but the Highland Ball continued until past one in the morning.

Next day was marked by a small ceremony and procession, as the Honours of Scotland were returned from Holyroodhouse up the Royal Mile to the Castle, accompanied by a Clan Macgregor Regalia Guard.

The King did not appear until that evening, attending a huge civic banquet given by the Lord Provost, Sir William Arbuthnot, in the great Hall of Parliament House which Murray had decorated with tapestries. When the guests had eaten their fill of turtle soup, stewed carp, grouse, venison, and apricot tart, accompanied by Moselle and Champagne, the hymn of thanksgiving, Non Nobis Domine, was sung and then the Lord Provost proposed the health of "His Majesty, who has been graciously pleased to honour us with his presence, The King, four times three."

After a rousing rendition of God Save the King, the King declared, "This is one of the proudest days of my life," and expressed his heart-felt thanks to the people of Scotland.

The next day His Majesty attended a service at St. Giles' Cathedral, where he was struck by the silence and decorum of the crowds.

On Monday 26th, the King made a private visit to the Holyroodhouse apartments of his ancestor Mary, Queen of Scots. The Palace had been hastily redecorated for the visit, but the old, faded, and disintegrating fabrics lent an air of neglect to her rooms. The King declared that the historic apartments should be preserved and maintained for posterity, insisting that the Government make a grant for the essential repairs needed.

King George made his last and least formal public appearance the following evening, when he attended a theatrical performance of Scott's Rob Roy in the Theatre Royal. It must have been quite an event. James Ballantyne reported in his newspaper that "the audience was closely wedged together, and the boxes were filled with the rank, wealth and beauty of Scotland". Sir Walter was "greeted with loud acclamations" and when the King appeared there was "a death-like stillness" before a "prolonged and heart-felt shout which, for more than a minute, rent the house."

The King heartily enjoyed the performance, following the play closely and laughing especially loudly at the wit and innocent sarcasms of Bailie Nicol Jarvie. The highlight for him was when the Bailie told Frank Osbaldiston that he would have "Nane o' your Lun'on tricks".

The royal visit ended on Thursday 29 August with a brief visit to Hopetoun House where elaborate arrangements had been made to serve a sumptuous lunch. The King, mindful that he was about to take to the North Sea, ate only turtle soup before conferring the honours of Knighthood on Captain Adam Ferguson, Deputy Keeper of the Scottish Regalia, and the painter Henry Raeburn. The programme complete, he joined the Royal yacht

"HMY Royal George" at nearby South Queensferry and set sail for home.

Just as it had been on the day of his arrival in the Forth the week before, the weather was wet for the crowds waiting to see the King off. Sir Walter declared, "it is right that Scotland should weep when parting with her good King."

Even with the level of detailed planning on which Sir Walter had insisted, the King's visit to Scotland had been a risky venture. But as he sailed off down the Firth of Forth, all those involved must have shared a sense of huge satisfaction and understandable relief. It had been a triumph, increasing goodwill within the Union and establishing a new-found Scottish national identity which continues to influence the way the world thinks about Scotland. Sir Walter's attention to detail when it came to the symbolism of events had united Highlander and Lowlander in ways that would previously have been unimaginable. The Highland Clan chieftains had initially resented what they saw as the controlling ways of Sir Walter, but now they revelled in a reinvigorated sense of heritage.

A lasting legacy of the King's visit was the appointment of the Royal Company of Archers as the "The King's Bodyguard in Scotland". He also presented the Captain General, The Earl of Hopetoun, with a Gold Stick to emphasise this formal recognition of the Royal Company's place in Scotland. This remains the title of this distinguished body to this day - changing to Queen's

Bodyguard when appropriate - and the Captain General has been known as Gold Stick ever since.

While the King was at Edinburgh Castle, Sir Walter had taken the opportunity to express regret that the mighty siege gun, Mons Meg, had been taken to London after the Jacobite rebellions. His Majesty was sympathetic and after a lengthy correspondence with the cannon's official guardians at the Tower of London, including the Duke of Wellington, the gun was returned to Edinburgh Castle in 1829, where she can still be seen.

A less obvious consequence of the visit was Scott's successful campaign to have the Scottish peerages, forfeited during the Jacobite rebellions of 1715 and 1745, restored. The symbolism of this decision was important and played well with the Scots.

Sir Walter Scott had pulled off a phenomenal triumph which reflected his many remarkable skills. He had transformed a nation's attitude to their King, and the King's attitude to his Scottish subjects. Scotland was changed forever by that visit.

Chapter Ten

In which Walter
settles into life as
a Border Laird.

Sir Walter Scott had long since proved himself a gentleman of many facets. He was congenial by nature and had worked hard to realise his dream of a country house with its own estate. He had a reputation as a generous and welcoming host at his homes in Edinburgh and especially at Abbotsford. An internationally acclaimed writer, father and husband, courtier and royal event planner, he was also a popular local Sheriff and now a Border laird – all roles in which he took great pleasure.

He had always been known as a patient, good-humoured man. It was he who had settled the hot-headed chums of his youth when arguments threatened to turn ugly. It was to him the men in his Yeomanry troop would turn for a light-hearted quip to cheer them up after the hard exercise of training. In his courtroom he dispensed justice with a human touch of understanding for the miscreants who came before him but also for their victims. He had managed a potentially truculent monarch with skill and diplomacy, creating a spectacle which had revived Scottish national pride and created a blueprint for showcasing Scotland to the world which still holds up today.

Despite all his achievements, Sir Walter was a modest man. When he was asked how he compared to Robert Burns, he replied sincerely, "there is no comparison whatever, we ought not to be named in the same day." On another occasion he would declare the poet and dramatist Joanna Baillie to be "the highest genius of our country."

It did not mean that there was no limit to Sir Walter's patience, only that he rarely reached it. As his fame grew, an increasing number of people wanted to claim his friendship and many came to visit him, with or without an invitation.

Some he welcomed, others he did not. Over the years he welcomed as guests to Abbotsford Prince Leopold, later King of the Belgians, Prince Gustavus of Sweden, the writers Maria Edgeworth and Thomas Moore, and the artist JMW Turner who travelled north to illustrate a new edition of Scott's poems. In 1817 he was delighted to receive an unexpected visit from the American writer Washington Irving who was passing Abbotsford on his way to view Melrose Abbey. Sir Walter had already read and enjoyed one of his works and was thrilled to meet him, pressing him to stay and showing him the Border countryside in the company of his family and his dogs.

There was nothing Sir Walter loved more than showing off the countryside of his ancestors, pointing out its romance and history in every sweep of its landscapes. He would often stop at a point high on Bemersyde hill overlooking the Tweed, known now as Scott's View. He loved this place, which drops away to a long, rich view of the valley of the River Tweed dominated in the distance by the three peaks of the Eildon hills. Local legend has it that Sir Walter stopped here so often on the way home to Abbotsford that his horses learned to halt without command.

In Edinburgh, Sir Walter liked to dine in the Clubs to which he still belonged, although in his later years he tired of having to listen to young Whig lawyers who only wanted to show off with convoluted arguments designed to show how clever they were, rather than to advance anybody's knowledge. In contrast, his son-in-law described Scott's conversational skill as "sunshine which gilds the most indifferent objects and adds brilliancy to the brightest."

Food was always one of Sir Walter's greatest pleasures. His tastes in food were said to be plain and Scottish. Scott wrote that he only ate twice a day, breakfast and a moderate dinner. At Abbotsford his breakfast, served about nine, is said to have been porridge with cream, salmon, a home-made ham, a pie, or a cold sheep's head, followed by oatcakes, or slices of brown bread spread thick with butter. Skipping lunch wouldn't have been such a hardship after a breakfast of that scale!

The hospitality at Abbotsford was lavish and Lady Scott would often chide her husband for overfeeding his guests. John Gibson Lockhart describes the fare after one Abbotsford Hunt in late October: "A baron of beef roasted, at the foot of the table, a salted round at the head, while tureens of hare soup, hotchpotch, and cockey-leekie extended down the centre, and such light articles as geese, turkeys, entire suckling pigs, a singed sheep's head, and the unfailing haggis, were set forth by way of side dishes. Blackcock and moorfowl, bushels of snipe, black puddings, white puddings, and pyramids of pancakes formed the second course. Ale was the favorite beverage during dinner, but there was plenty of port and sherry for those whose stomachs they suited. The quaichs of Glenlivet, (Sir Walter preferred whisky to wine), were filled brimful and tossed off as if they held water. The wine decanters made a few rounds of the table but the hints for hot punch and toddy soon became clamorous."

Sir Walter's novels are scattered with descriptions of meals, some elaborate with a bewildering variety of dishes and others simple with meagre fare. Most of the meals are Scottish but there are some from English tables too. All betray Scott's abiding interest in food and are most likely to be inspired by the many meals he had enjoyed in the company of his numerous friends.

In Old Mortality for example, Scott describes how "old Robin, who was butler, valet-de-chambre, footman, gardener, and what not, in the house of Milnwood, placed on the table an immense charger of broth, thickened with oatmeal and colewort, in which ocean of liquid was indistinctly discovered, by close observers, two or three short ribs of lean mutton sailing to and fro. Two huge baskets, one of bread made of barley and pease, and one of oatcakes, flanked this standing dish. A large, boiled salmon would now-a-days have indicated more liberal house-keeping; but at that period salmon was caught in such plenty in the considerable rivers in Scotland, that instead of being accounted a delicacy, it was generally applied to feed the servants, who are said sometimes to have stipulated that they should not be required to eat a food so luscious and surfeiting in its quality above five times a-week. The large black jack, filled with very small beer of Milnwood's own brewing, was allowed to the company at discretion, as were the bannocks, cakes, and broth; but the mutton was reserved for the heads of the family and a measure of ale, somewhat deserving the name, was set apart in a silver tankard for their exclusive use. A huge kebbock, (a cheese, that is, made with ewemilk mixed with cow's milk,) and a jar of salt butter, were in common to the company."

Scott is even believed to have been instrumental in the publication of one of Scotland's most important culinary works, *The Cook and Housewife's Manual*, published in Edinburgh in 1826 under the pseudonym of Mistress Margaret Dods, a character in Scott's 1824 novel *St Ronan's Well*. It is a fascinating record of culinary traditions, customs, and old national dishes with such evocative names as Inky Pinky, Cabbie Claw, Venison Collops, Friar's Chicken, Bashed Neeps, Cock-A-Leekie, Stoved Chicken, and Howtowdie.

The introduction to the cookbook is, effectively, a short story, widely believed to have been written by Sir Walter himself. It describes the meeting of a gourmet club at the Cleikum Inn, including many of the characters from *St Ronan's Well*. The main body of the book is full of witty comments and a lively discussion on the culinary arts. More importantly, it was the first to record Scotland's cuisine. Full of hundreds of Scottish recipes, there are also detailed sections on frying, roasting and baking as well as chapters on housekeeping and medicine-making. Although always known as Meg Dods Cookery, the book – apart from the introduction - was actually compiled and written by Isobel Christian Johnstone.

Sir Walter found it difficult to resist the temptation to buy more and more land to expand the Abbotsford estate. His ambitions for the place were entirely good-hearted, if economically unwise. He took seriously his responsibility to make the countryside, "a more beautiful and aesthetically pleasing place in which folk of every station could work and live at their ease."

He believed strongly that the best landowners and landlords dwelt at home and spent their money on their estates and their tenants, instead of, as he put it, "cutting a figure in France or Italy".

He was an enlightened landlord and employer, introducing a system of health insurance and replacing the easy path of simply handing out money to people in short-term distress, preferring the option of relief work at full wages. He proposed a scheme of unemployment insurance in factories, the premiums to be paid wholly by the owners, to hold them back from reckless expansion without regard for the need to keep their workers in employment and earning.

Scott may have been a progressive thinker, but he was not a social reformer in any self-righteous sense. He had the healthy regard of the countryman for a fair reward for fair labour, and always regarded farming as the most serious occupation a country gentleman might have. He took a keen interest in the way in which some estate owners had managed nature to form pleasant surroundings for their houses, but he was critical of the way in which many, though not all, landowners tinkered with the natural world and made a mess of it. He particularly regretted the passing of the deer parks which had long been a feature of many established estates. These woods had been carefully laid out to represent a natural forest and encourage the deer within them to feel at home, as well as providing guests with quiet places to walk if they wanted a bit of peace.

At Abbotsford, Sir Walter made his own limited but effective efforts to practise what he preached. The walls around his garden were (and still are) a warm brick and there was (and is) a small building, an open glasshouse, in which he and his guests could sit in the heat of the day or the cool of the evening and enjoy the beds of flowers spread on the slope before them. Sir Walter believed that the owners of gardens needed to lavish attention on them. Without constant work, they would change beyond recognition, turning places of beauty and tranquillity into ruins.

Beyond his stunning garden Scott looked to his great love of trees. "Trees remain the proper and most manageable material of picturesque improvement," he wrote in an essay on the planting of wastelands, "and as trees and bushes can be raised almost anywhere, as by their presence they not only delight the eye, with their various forms and colours, but benefit the soil by their falling leaves, and improve the climate by their shelter, there is scarcely any property fitted for human habitation so utterly hopeless, as not to be rendered agreeable by extensive and judicious plantations."

He visited landowners up and down the country, probing

their land-management methods and learning from their successes and mistakes. He worked this expertise into his writing too. In *Heart of Midlothian*, he included this exhortation of the dying Scotch laird to his son: "Be aye sticking in a tree, Jock—it will be growing whilst you are sleeping."

It is little wonder that Sir Walter's observations of nature found their way into his books and poems. His descriptions of the countryside are everywhere. Open virtually any of his books and you will read careful descriptions of the landscapes through which the actions of his stories are taking place.

But as the world looked on admiringly at the ageing Shirra, constantly busy, surrounded by friends and family, disaster was silently eating away at the foundations of those triumphs.

Chapter Eleven

In which Abbotsford
is finished at last,
but Sir Walter
suffers money troubles
and personal loss.

Organising a royal visit and being an expert on tree planting was not enough to slow Sir Walter's pen. Besides his novels, and before them his poems, he also did his best to meet the endless requests for essays on such subjects as varied as *Chivalry*, the *Planting of Wastelands*, the *Feudal System*, and the Drama, for Prefaces and copious notes on other writers. He found it hard to say no, but still managed to produce a prolific crop of new novels.

Throughout 1822, the busy year of the King's visit to Scotland, Sir Walter was completing *Peveril of the Peak* and it was published at the start of 1823. He immediately moved on to the rollicking tale *of Quentin Durward* which was published later in 1823. That novel, set in France, centres on the rivalry between King Louis XI and the Duke of Burgundy. Quentin, whose uncle is one of the Scottish archer guards of the King, is in France to seek military service and performs the various complex tasks given to him with good sense and gallantry. The tale met with a tepid reaction from readers in Britain but when it took Paris by storm, it was suddenly acclaimed as a great story and became a roaring success in Britain too.

St Ronan's Well was published in 1824. It is his only novel set in the Border country of Tweeddale and the only one set in his own nineteenth century. Saint Ronan's Well is a spa in the Border town of Innerleithen. In contrast to the sweep of adventure and the glamour of pageantry in previous books, this one dwells on life's ironies. The novel concerns the tragic rivalry of Valentine Bulmer, the Earl of Etherington, and his half-brother Francis Tyrrel who both wish to marry Miss Clara Mowbray. Among its characters it introduces the incomparable Meg Dods, who runs the Cleikum Inn where both protagonists had stayed, and who, as mentioned previously, would be named as the supposed author of the famous *Meg Dods' Cookery Book*.

When that novel was finished, Scott began *Redgauntlet* which reached the public in June 1824. In this story he returned to the border country between Scotland and England and the Solway Firth of Guy Mannering. Set after the Rebellion of '45, Hugh Redgauntlet plots to set off a new Jacobite rebellion and kidnaps the book's hero, Darsie Latimer, to force him to join the rebels. The plot is uncovered and the plotters, including Prince Charles Edward Stuart, who had slipped back into Scotland, are exiled and the hero is set free. It is not high adventure but draws the characters into a web in which they are carried to an unavoidable fate.

Twelve years after they had moved into the unimpressive farmhouse at Cartley Hole, in the autumn of 1824, Abbotsford was finally finished. Among the gifts that arrived to mark the event were 15 volumes of Bernard de Montfaucon's *Antiquities* bound in scarlet morocco leather from the King. Into the new entrance hall went the heavier parts of the old armour which Scott had collected over so many years, along with sundry skins, horns, and assorted objects. They included the sword presented to the great Marquis of Montrose by King Charles I with Prince Henry's arms and cypher on one side of the blade and the King's on the other, and a quaich with a glass bottom which had belonged to Prince Charles Edward Stuart.

That October brought some sadness too, with the death of Scott's "noblest and most celebrated hound" Maida. He was buried by the porch of Abbotsford, his grave marked by a "louping on" stone, carved by Scott's master-mason, John Smith, with the recumbent figure of the dog. To it was added the Latin inscription, translated as:

Beneath the sculptured form which late you wore
Sleep soundly, Maida, at your master's door.

There was a memorable housewarming that Christmas with a larger than ever party and the house resounded to singing and the declaiming of poems and ballads.

As 1825 began, a grand ball was held at Abbotsford to celebrate the engagement of the Scotts' elder son, Lt Walter Scott, to Miss Jane Jobson. The couple were married on 3rd February in Edinburgh.

As the year wore on, Sir Walter completed *Tales of the Crusaders*, *The Betrothed*, and *The Talisman*. Set at the end of the Third Crusade, this story was roughly based on the curious healing properties of the Lee Penny. This magical charm, a dark red semi-precious stone, was reputed to provide a remedy against bleeding and fever, rabies and sickness in horses and cattle. It was brought to Scotland by Sir Simon Lockhart during the crusades of the 14th century as part of the ransom of a Moorish Amir. Later it was set in a silver fourpenny piece from the reign of King Edward the Fourth and kept in a gold snuffbox given to the Lockhart family of Lee Castle near Lanark by the Austrian Empress Maria Theresa. In Sir Walter's story *Saladin*, posing as a Muslim healer, cures King Richard the Lionheart of a fever using the Lee Penny.

It is clear from hints which Sir Walter dropped at the time that he wanted to write history. He had been fascinated by Napoleon Bonaparte and had read volumes about him as they appeared. He was used to reading widely and then applying his imagination to what he had in his head, but a biography of the *Life of Napoleon* required him to be precise and to spend hours going through documents and making meticulous notes of fact rather than of fancy. Wagon loads of documents arrived at his Edinburgh house and his friends scoured every source at home and abroad for written material. Originally the biography was planned to fill four volumes, but it was soon clear that this would not do that particular life justice, and in the end the complete work ran to nine volumes. Sir Walter went to Paris to pursue his research and on the way home sought at length the views of the Duke of Wellington on the man whose army he had finally defeated at Waterloo. The book was a prodigious feat written at speed, but gratifyingly to Scott, when it was published in June 1827 the public liked it, and it brought in some much-needed funds to the Scott coffers.

This was important because it was during the period in which he was writing the biography that Sir Walter realised he could no longer ignore the cold draught of financial troubles creeping under their door.

Since his first decision in 1809 to help out his old school friend James Ballantyne by taking a secret partnership in the Ballantyne printing business, Scott had continued to support him and various other people; he was a successful writer and could afford to be generous. However, there were those who had taken advantage of his good nature and owed him money. He had also borrowed heavily, using the backing of such patrons as the Duke of Buccleuch, building up a large number of IOUs over the years, which he set against projected earnings from his future writing. It was a big gamble.

In 1825 that gamble failed spectacularly. Investors had become greedy, speculating in increasingly fantastic schemes, which they believed promised higher and higher returns. When these failed to deliver and the stock market crashed, a financial panic took hold. The Bank of England was only saved from complete catastrophe with gold from the Banque de France. Six London and sixty country banks in England collapsed.

The crisis had a direct effect on the publishing industry. Those publishers who were in the habit of offering authors handsome advances were often in debt to banks and other creditors and many, including Constable and Co, Ballantynes and Scott's London agents Hurst and Robinson, who had speculated unwisely based on Scott's credit, collapsed and were forced to declare bankruptcy.

It took some time for the reality of the perilous state of the money-market to hit Sir Walter and his loyal son-in-law Lockhart. The banks headed up the queues of creditors as they pursued their money down the complicated chain of previous dealings, many of which stopped at Scott. But by that point the great writer had finally run out of funds.

It had taken many years, but eventually his generous but unwise financial commitments had caught up with him. It was a terrible shock, but, typically, Scott did not pull out his handkerchief and feel sorry for himself. His immediate concern was for the calamity he had brought on his family, his staff, and his dogs.

Some – although not all - of his friends rallied round. The politician and later Foreign Secretary Lord Dudley wrote "let every man to whom Sir Walter Scott has given months of delight give him a sixpence and he will rise tomorrow morning richer than Rothschild". Some even thought the government should step in. But Scott blamed no-one but himself and would take no charity; he most certainly would not slide away from his responsibilities by declaring himself legally bankrupt.

Scott was now 55, but he was determined to face with honour whatever the future might hold. He would work off what he owed in however many years remained to him. "My own right hand shall pay my debt," he declared.

A Trust was formed which helped to ease the immediate financial pressure on the Scotts by securing for them the occupancy of Abbotsford and the estate rent-free. And Sir Walter still had his income as the local Sheriff and the Clerk to the Court of Session.

He sold his Edinburgh house, the proceeds of which went towards paying off some of his debts and settled down in

Abbotsford with his wife, his daughter Anne, a reduced staff, and his beloved dogs. But this new way of living was not to bring him comfort.

At the start of their long marriage of close to 30 years, Scott had praised his wife Charlotte's "good sense and good education". It was an opinion he never changed. He had come to rely on the "studious neatness" of this kindly, humorous woman to run their friendly and hospitable homes in Edinburgh, Lasswade, Ashestiel and latterly at Abbotsford. She was, he wrote, "the faithful and true companion of my fortunes good and bad for so many years". Unfortunately, however, she had grown seriously ill. Her constitution had been sound, but she had developed a breathlessness which indicated that there were further complications.

There was good news when Scott's elder daughter Sophia gave birth to another grandson in April 1826. He was christened Walter. Anne, the Scotts' youngest child, continued to nurse her mother who slept a great deal, drifting in and out of awareness. Sir Walter returned to Edinburgh and his court work as his wife's illness wore on, only to be given the terrible news on 15th May that his wife had died that morning, most likely of pneumonia. The Shirra hurried straight back from the capital.

Charlotte's death left Sir Walter shattered and for the first time he allowed some self-pity. "I think my heart will break. Lonely, aged, deprived of my family all but poor Anne, impoverished, an embarrassed man, I am deprived of the sharer of my thoughts and counsels … which must break the heart that must bear them alone. Even her foibles were of service to me by giving me things to think of beyond my weary self-reflection."

Charlotte was buried in the peaceful precincts of the ruined Dryburgh Abbey on a beautiful day. Her husband helped bear her coffin to the grave, stood beside it in silence throughout the ceremony, then solemnly bowed to the assembled company and without a word entered his carriage and was driven home.

Afterwards "the solitude seemed so absolute. My poor Charlotte would have been in the room half a score of times to see if the fire burned and to ask a hundred kind questions," Scott wrote in the Journal which he had started the year before.

As time went on, Anne, who had been worn out by the strain of nursing her mother, began to recover her strength, and the man who had given the world more stories and more memorable characters than any other, picked up his pen and started on the immense task of writing his way out of debt.

First, he drove himself to complete *Woodstock* which is set just after the English Civil War when Oliver Cromwell had executed King Charles and created his Commonwealth, turning Great Britain and Ireland into a republic. Inspired by the legend of the Good Devil of Woodstock, which supposedly tormented Cromwellian parliamentary commissioners who had taken possession of a royal residence, the story deals with the escape of King Charles the Second in 1652 and his final triumphant entry into London in 1660. The novel was published in 1826.

In 1827, Sir Walter took the chair at a dinner of the Theatrical Fund and allowed Lord Meadowbank, in proposing his health, to publicly admit, finally, that the author of *Waverley* was indeed Sir Walter Scott. Although it had long been an open secret, the news was still received with wild applause.

Sir Walter may not have appreciated it at the time, but the sensible Robert Cadell, his publisher's former business partner, revived an idea which would eventually clear his debts. Cadell had re-established himself in business following his own bankruptcy and wanted to publish all of the *Waverley* novels with new annotations and revisions by Scott and illustrations by the artist J.M.W Turner in a 48-volume set.

The ambitious plan turned out to be the success Cadell had predicted and played a major part in clearing Sir Walter's debts. The sad thing is that he didn't live long enough to know it.

Despite his immediate troubles, Scott's political antennae remained finely tuned and his persuasive skills were undimmed. He saw the political risks north of the border in a proposal by the government, frightened by the financial crisis, that private banks should no longer print their own banknotes. He responded with a hugely effective pamphlet, *Letters of Malachi Malagrowther*, which killed off the proposal in Scotland. Writing to his friend John

Wilson Croker MP and Secretary to the Admiralty, who had opposed Scott's views, he said, "If you unscotch us you will find us damned mischievous Englishmen." Sir Walter still appears on all Bank of Scotland notes to commemorate this success.

Although the biography of Napoleon was selling well, Scott felt he could not afford to rest. Under the umbrella title of *Chronicles of the Canongate* he wrote *Chrystal Croftangry's Narrative* with two short stories. After the grand sweep of his huge biography of Napoleon, *The Highland Widow* and *The Two Drovers* saw him return to a more homely style. *The Surgeon's Daughter* followed in a separate volume.

By 1828, Sir Walter was beginning to recover his health and his spirits and set to work on the second set of the *Chronicles* with *The Fair Maid of Perth*. This novel is set in the late fourteenth century when the son of King Robert III attempts to abduct Catharine Glover, the 'Fair Maid of Perth', and the plot revolves around the true but misty story of the Battle of the Clans on the North Inch of Perth in 1396. Happily for Scott, it was received with wide critical approval.

Still driving himself hard, in 1829 he hurried on with the next book, *Anne of Geierstein*, set in the period following *Quentin Durward*. It follows two exiled Englishmen hoping to gain the help of the Duke of Burgundy in regaining the English crown. They get into difficulties in the Swiss mountains where they meet Countess Anne and her family who are involved in the politics of the newly independent Swiss Confederation. The novel's historical backdrop was drawn from the deep wells of Sir Walter's memory. He was writing under immense pressure.

Early the following year he returned from his work at the Court and fainted at his daughter's feet. He briefly lost his ability to speak but recovered it fairly quickly and was up and about again in a day or two. He complained that his lameness was getting worse and eventually was forced to wear "an apparatus" to help him walk.

Scott had survived so many health emergencies over the years, but he was aware that the grim reaper was stalking him. "Such a shaking hands with death was formidable," he declared with characteristic aplomb, but he "should not care for all this if I was sure of dying handsomely".

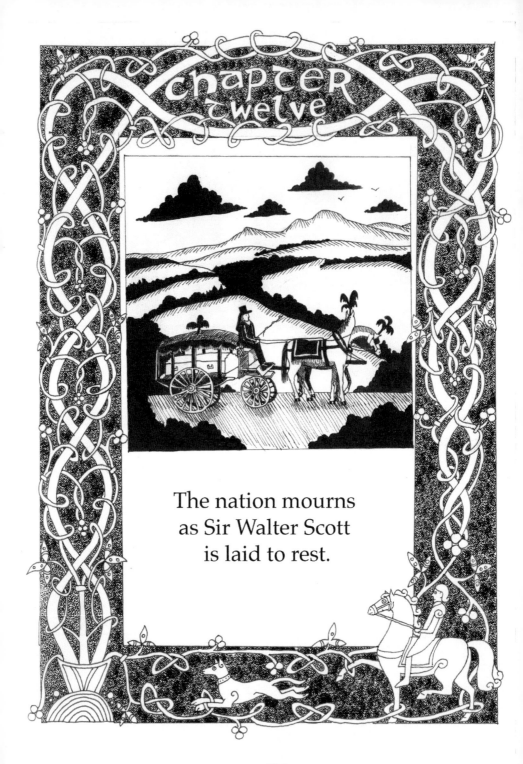

Chapter Twelve

The nation mourns
as Sir Walter Scott
is laid to rest.

Sir Walter tried to shrug off the health warning, but he could not shrug off the sadness which came with the steady passing of old friends.

In October of 1829 he received the bitter blow of the unexpected death of Tom Purdie, his "humble and sincere friend". Tom had seemed in perfectly good health but one evening laid his head on his arms and seemed to be asleep. When his family tried to stir him later, he did not respond. After he had arranged the burial of his "old and faithful servant, my factotum" in a grave close to Melrose Abbey, Scott returned to Edinburgh, keen to be away from Abbotsford with all its memories.

Sir Walter reckoned that it would take two more years before his debts were cleared and set to work again on another novel in the *Tales of My Landlord* series, *Count Robert of Paris*. Count Robert was a Frankish knight who disrupted negotiations between the leaders of the First Crusade and the Byzantine Emperor Komnenos by occupying the throne when it was temporarily vacant.

None of his close friends liked the early chapters, so Sir Walter laid them aside to tackle what he saw as a new political iniquity. The government of the Duke of Wellington had fallen, and the new government of Earl Grey proposed a Reform Act which extended the vote to a vastly increased number of people. Sir Walter heartily disapproved of the change, and at a meeting in Jedburgh described the Government as like "a parcel of schoolboys taking to pieces a watch which used to go tolerably well … in the conceit that they can put it together again far better than the old watchmaker. I fear that they will fail because their first step had been to break the mainspring." But for once in his life, he had misjudged the mood of the public and was greeted with violent hissing and hooting. On election day a band of weavers from Hawick shouted insults at him, his carriage was stoned, and a woman spat at him. When Parliament eventually passed the Reform Act by one vote Sir Walter's response was, "Sed transeat. It is vain to mourn what cannot be mended."

Scott turned his attention back to *Castle Dangerous*, the last novel to be published during his lifetime. It is set at t he time of the Wars of Independence around 1306, shortly after the death of William Wallace. It was a story which Scott had long had in his head, and he was anxious to commit it to paper. Castle Dangerous was a Castle of the Black Douglas on the border between Ayrshire and Lanarkshire which had been captured by the English. After various attempts to retake the castle by subversion, word comes that the English army has been routed by Robert the Bruce and the fortress is returned to the Douglas family.

The doctors insisted Sir Walter rest from the incessant work, and they had their way when Scott finally agreed to seek some rest and sunshine. The government of Lord Grey, which Scott had so vigorously opposed over the Reform Act, generously put the frigate HMS Barham at his disposal.

At the end of October 1831, after a short delay because of the weather, Sir Walter, with his daughter Anne and his son Walter, sailed south from Portsmouth past Trafalgar and Gibraltar and docked at the Mediterranean island of Malta. Their stay inspired Scott to begin a novel set against the backdrop of the great Siege of Malta when the Knights of St John beat back a siege by a vastly superior number of Ottoman Turks in 1565.

The Knights had originally set up a hospital in Jerusalem in the 11th century to treat pilgrims making the long trek to the Holy Land. After the rise of Islam across the Middle East and North Africa, the Muslim leaders drove the Knights out of Jerusalem, first to Cyprus, then Rhodes and finally to Malta where they were established for 268 years. Malta was a strategically placed base and the Ottoman Turks decided to attack the island and drive the Christian Knights right out of the Mediterranean with a force of some 40,000 men. The Knights, who numbered around 6,000 under their Grand Master Jean de Valette, withstood the Ottoman siege for nearly four months, finally driving them back to Turkey. Eventually, in 1798, the Knights were expelled by Napoleon but bequeathed to the island their eight-pointed cross, now best known as a Maltese Cross; the name of their Grand Master for the Capital city Valetta; and many fine buildings which the Knights had built to house a hospital, a library, and a University.

After three weeks there, the Barham sailed on to Naples, where Sir Walter's son Charles was attaché to the British Embassy, and where he stayed for four months. He enjoyed visiting the tourist sights, where he was often recognised. Wearing his Royal Company of Archers uniform, he met King Ferdinand II. The pair spoke to each other for a while, but Sir Walter later said that he doubted if either understood a word the other had said.

He set about collecting Neapolitan ballads, spending time every day working on his novel about the Siege of Malta. He confided to Sir William Gell, a Briton living in Naples, that he had inadvertently thrown part of it in the fire but had rewritten it better. By the time he left the city, he had nearly completed the novel, and a short story entitled *Bizarro* about the death of a local bandit known as Il Bizarro.

Years of precarious health were taking their toll, and his fellow travellers began to notice that Sir Walter was slipping in and out of a closed world of his own.

He had planned to go on to the Austrian Tyrol in April 1832 to visit the German poet Goethe at Weimar. When news reached him that Goethe had died at home the previous month, it seemed to set back all his hopes of recovery and he decided that he must return to Abbotsford immediately.

Young Walter had already left to return to his regiment in early March, but Charles Scott was given leave to accompany his father home. The party set off by carriage, pausing in Rome to see the tombs of Bonnie Prince Charlie. Sir Walter, impatient to get home, was unexcited by Venice, Austria, Bavaria, the Rhineland and the Netherlands, refusing to visit sights which would have delighted him in earlier days. At one inn Sir Walter signed himself "Sir Walter Scott – for Scotland". When he reached

London, he had another seizure but was determined to return to Abbotsford, and so in July 1822 he arrived home for the last time.

His spirits revived as soon as he saw the familiar surroundings of the home he had built. That summer he rested in a bed brought down to the bay window of his dining room. From there he could see the River Tweed and hear the comforting sounds of the river and the birds in the trees which he had so lovingly planted. Sadly however, this did little to stop his health gradually weakening further until, surrounded by his family, he died there on Friday the 21st of September 1832.

Five days later the body of Scotland's greatest storyteller was taken from Abbotsford to Dryburgh Abbey near St Boswells. Huge crowds turned out to line the way, people standing silent and bareheaded as the hearse and funeral procession passed. Behind the three hundred invited mourners came a great throng of people who might not have received invitations but wanted to pay the illustrious Sir Walter their respects nonetheless.

The day was dark and windy with the sky threatening rain, but as the long procession reached the point on Bemersyde Hill known as Scott's View, the horses drawing the hearse stopped as they had been accustomed in their master's lifetime.

At Dryburgh, his household staff bore his coffin to the graveside into the care of the pallbearers: his sons Walter and Charles, son-in-law John Gibson Lockhart and six-year-old grandson Walter, with seven others including his cousins and the Chief of his family, Lord Polwarth. The great man was laid to rest beside his wife within the peaceful ruins of the old Abbey.

In Edinburgh it was decided to honour Sir Walter Scott with one of the biggest monuments to a writer anywhere in the world. In 1840, work began on a gothic-style memorial towering over 200 feet, which still dominates the centre of the Scottish capital. The view of the city from the top is worth the climb up the steep spiral staircase. As soon as the idea was announced donations poured in from all over the United Kingdom and beyond. The monument displayed the heads of other writers and important names from Scottish history as well as figures of many of the characters from Scott's books and poems. A marble statue of Scott with Maida at his feet was sculpted by the Scottish artist Sir John Steell to sit in the centre, at the foot of the monument.

Glasgow also decided to honour the great writer with a statue, sculpted by John Greenshields, which stands on top of a handsome 24 metre pillar in the centre of George Square. It was completed in 1837, before Edinburgh's monument, and towers above the Square's other figures including the mounted statues of Queen Victoria and Prince Albert.

There are statues of Sir Walter Scott outside his courtroom in Selkirk, at nearby Clovenfords and in Parliament Hall in Edinburgh. A fine bronze of The Shirra, a copy of the statue in the Scott Monument, sits at the southern end of the Literary Walk in New York's Central Park.

Through the romantic and dramatic images against which he set his hugely popular poems and novels and, of course, in promoting tartan as Scotland's national dress, Sir Walter Scott is widely credited with presenting Scotland as a tourist destination across the world. His first novel *Waverley* gave its name to Edinburgh's main railway station and indeed the entire line between Edinburgh and Carlisle. A class of locomotives was also named after the novel and another after Luckie Mucklebackit in *The Antiquary*. There are more than 90 streets commemorating him and his work in Britain alone and many more around the Commonwealth and far beyond. The little steamer on Loch Katrine in the Trossachs, where the *Lady of the Lake* was set, named the Sir Walter Scott, still transports tourists to this day. Even a breed of dog, the Dandie Dinmont, was named after a character in *Guy Mannering*.

But his lasting legacy is his writing. The long ballads and the *Waverley Novels* were written before there was radio or television, cinema, or the internet, when travel was cumbersome, often uncomfortable, and slow. Sir Walter Scott gave the public, hungry for a fresh view of the world, stories which carried them far beyond their own imaginations. His novels and poems have gone on to inspire some 90 operas including Rossini's *La Donna del Lago*, Donizetti's *Lucia di Lammermoor*, Hamish McCunn's *Jeanie Deans*, Georges Bizet's *The Fair Maid of Perth* and plays such as *Rob Roy*. Composers, including Schubert and Beethoven, have set his songs to music, and dozens of artists have painted scenes inspired by his novels, many of them displayed in major galleries.

For today's consumers, Scott's novels can seem difficult to read. When put in context of the times – over two hundred years ago, remember - the history and vivid characters to be discovered in his stories are a wonderful reminder of why Sir Walter Scott's legacy is so important. His knowledge and interest in Scottish folk tales and oral traditions have prevented their loss to time and memory and are an incredibly important part of Scotland's literary history.

He is truly Scotland's Greatest Storyteller.

About the Author

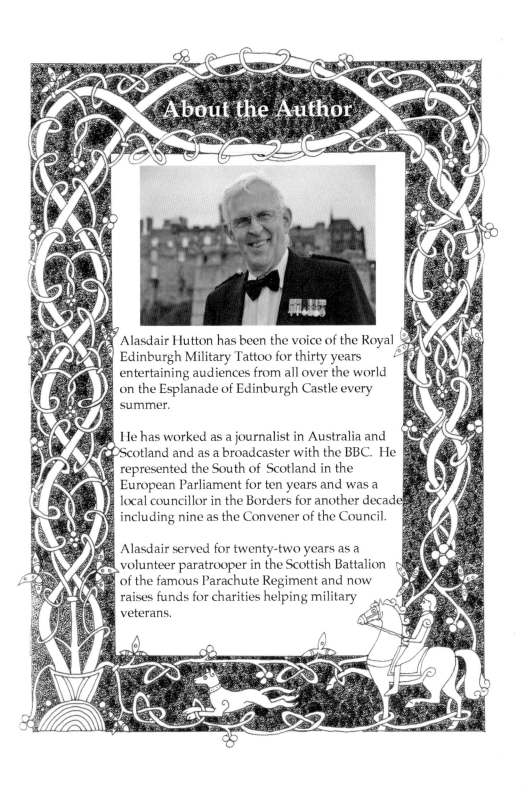

Alasdair Hutton has been the voice of the Royal Edinburgh Military Tattoo for thirty years entertaining audiences from all over the world on the Esplanade of Edinburgh Castle every summer.

He has worked as a journalist in Australia and Scotland and as a broadcaster with the BBC. He represented the South of Scotland in the European Parliament for ten years and was a local councillor in the Borders for another decade including nine as the Convener of the Council.

Alasdair served for twenty-two years as a volunteer paratrooper in the Scottish Battalion of the famous Parachute Regiment and now raises funds for charities helping military veterans.

ACKNOWLEDGEMENTS

This little book was a labour of love, a bow of respect to the greatest storyteller Scotland has produced, Sir Walter Scott, two hundred and fifty years after he was born.

Although he contracted polio as an infant he did not let it hold him back from doing whatever he chose to do. He had an extraordinary gift of imagination which brought forth a vivid procession of characters peopling a bewildering range of stories in poems and novels and that was not all.

He was a successful lawyer, a volunteer soldier, a peacemaker, a keen forester and a collector of the lore of the Borderland which may well have been forgotten if he had not captured it before it vanished quietly away.

I took a long time to pluck up the courage to take up the challenge of Lindsey Fraser to write a short history of Sir Walter for young people and those who had not yet opened one of his books. There is a common perception that Scott is too old fashioned and full of excessive language to be read and appreciated by readers in the twenty first century who are accustomed to brief sound-bites and do not have the attention span to manage a whole Scott novel.

This is a shallow way dismiss a master storyteller. I hope more readers will have the courage to turn their backs on these nay-sayers and step out on a series of remarkable adventures which will richly reward each journey.

Although I have always appreciated Scott's skill, I am deeply grateful to Lindsey Fraser for her push in the back which set me writing and then her quite remarkable skill as an editor which transformed a pig's ear into something closer to a silk purse by comparison.

I am grateful to Lindsey Fraser and her brother Graham for the time they spent checking the text and taking out my silly mistakes. Those that remain are all mine and for those I must apologise to you and to the shade of Sir Walter. I must also thank Shalla Gray for having the courage to make Sir Walter's life available to younger and less familiar readers.

I am also most grateful to the many writers whose works I have consulted trying to piece together the threads of Sir Walter's remarkable and varied life. And most of all I am grateful to Sir Walter Scott for all he wrote and all that he achieved in his all too short 61 years.

Thank you, Sir Walter, this is my tiny homage to you.

Alasdair Hutton

Also by Alasdair Hutton for younger readers:

Mustard & Pepper

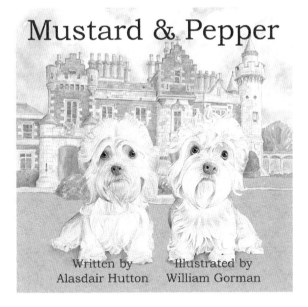

Written by
Alasdair Hutton

Illustrated by
William Gorman

Curly Tale Books titles you may also like:

ISBN: 978-1-9996336-84
Published by Curly Tale Books Ltd
34 Main Street
Kirkcowan
DG8 0HG
www.curlytalebooks.co.uk
Printed by J&B Print,
32A Albert Street, Newton Stewart, DG8 6EJ